SUFFOLK ARTISTS 1750-1930

*Paintings from the Ipswich Borough
Museums & Galleries Collection*

by Chlöe Bennett

IMAGES PUBLICATIONS & IPSWICH BOROUGH COUNCIL

SUFFOLK ARTISTS　　COPYRIGHT　©　IMAGES PUBLICATIONS & IPSWICH BOROUGH COUNCIL

Text Copyright © Chlöe Bennett 1991

Paintings courtesy Ipswich Borough Museums & Galleries Collection

First published in Great Britain 1991 by Images Publications
Woolpit, Suffolk IP30 9RP

Printed by Jolly & Barber Limited
Hillmorton Road, Rugby, Warwickshire CV22 5AN

Phototypeset by Roda Typographics Limited
29-35 Farringdon Road, London EC1M 3JB
Telephone: 071-430 1272

ISBN 0 948134 27 5 *(Paperback)*
ISBN 0 948134 28 3 *(Hardback)*

Front Cover:
Eleanor M. Every (1864-1935)
Cornfields near Kersey, Suffolk c1900

Chlöe Bennett

Chlöe Bennett B.A., M.Phil., A.M.A., is the Senior Assistant Curator (Humanities) at Ipswich Borough Museums & Galleries and has been responsible for the Fine and Decorative Art collections since 1979.

Born at Islington, London in 1953 and educated at Creighton Comprehensive School Muswell Hill, she went on to the University of Leicester where both of her degrees specialised in the History of Art. She has developed a knowledge of British provincial artists in Yorkshire as well as Suffolk. She has recently written *The Triumphant Image: Tudor & Stuart Portraits at Christchurch Mansion, Ipswich* and *The River Orwell: Artists' Views of Ipswich and its Waterfront over Two Centuries.*

Her prime concern has been to increase public access to museum collections and so it is appropriate that the publication of this book should coincide with the opening of the new **Suffolk Artists Gallery** at Christchurch Mansion, Ipswich.

Preface

This book presents an illustrated guide to the lives and activities of painters who worked in Suffolk from 1750 to 1930, and to the establishments, fashions and ideas which influenced their art. It does not aim to be a comprehensive dictionary of Suffolk artists, nor does it try to discuss every artist who has lived and worked in the county. Suffolk artists are defined, in this book, as those who strongly identified with the place and those who produced a substantial body of work here. Casual visitors or artists who happened to be born in Suffolk, never to return, are not included.

For the first time, Suffolk artists are drawn together as a distinct group, ranging from those of international repute, such as Thomas Gainsborough, John Constable, Philip Wilson Steer and Alfred Munnings to lesser known figures like Edward and Thomas Smythe, John Moore, Frederic George Cotman, Walter Batley, Harry Becker, Anna Airy and Rose Mead. New research has been combined with published sources. Bibliographies and references have been provided to enable further studies to be pursued by others in this neglected field.

Some artists who have not been selected on this occasion, especially those connected with modern art movements after 1930, will be covered in volume II of this series *Suffolk Landscapes* and possibly other publications based on the Ipswich collections.

Biographies of artists, placed beside each plate, are given in order of their date of birth. All of the paintings, reproduced in this volume, are from the Ipswich Borough Museums & Galleries collection and many have not been published before.

Introduction

The Suffolk Landscape Painters after Gainsborough

The landscapes of **Thomas Gainsborough** were a source of pride and inspiration to many artists working in Suffolk after his death. The Sudbury born artist, after a period of training in London under Hubert Gravelot (1699-1773), had settled in Ipswich from 1752 to 1759 before moving on to greater career prospects in fashionable Bath. His early Suffolk landscapes had been influenced by Dutch seventeenth century masters such as Jacob Ruisdael and Jan Wijnants. Their treatment of warm lighting and dramatic weather effects had elevated the flat farm lands and waterways of the Netherlands to a new scenic importance. The Suffolk terrain supplied Gainsborough with plenty of comparable natural subjects to sketch and paint, and a model scenery which could be used in creating his pastoral fantasies. Whereas in his portraits Gainsborough attained true likenesses of the sitters, he was not interested in producing topographical accuracy. In Suffolk, cartographic representations of ancient ruins, stately homes, churches and the like were undertaken by topographers such as Joshua Kirby (1716-1774), Francis Grose (c.1731-1791) and Isaac Johnson (1754-1835). This tradition was continued by Henry Davy (1793-1865) and other artists throughout the nineteenth century. Gainsborough's originality lay in his combination of Dutch naturalism and pictorial structure, the freer painterly rhythms of French masters such as Antoine Watteau and his own observation of the special unifying qualities of English light on the landscape.

John Constable's early amateur studies, with the encouragement of the artist J. T. Smith, included copying the work of Gainsborough, whom Smith had met, and the Dutch masters. Intrigued by the activities of Gainsborough in Ipswich he was able to write to his "tutor" in 1797 about "a place up the riverside where he often sat to sketch, on account of the beauty of the landscape, its extensiveness, and richness in variety, both in the fore and backgrounds". The letter noted "Smart and Frost (two drawing masters in Ipswich) often go there now to take views". He was undoubtedly referring to John Smart (1752/3-1838) the portrait painter and **George Frost** who frequented the spot by the River Orwell which became known as Gainsborough Lane, the steep path leading down to Piper's Vale. Frost was an enthusiastic collector and copyist of Gainsborough's pictures through which he developed a similar sketching technique. He may have influenced Constable, with whom he went out sketching on at least one occasion at Stoke Mills around 1805. Constable's veneration for Gainsborough was expressed again in 1799 when from Ipswich he wrote "'Tis a most delightfull country for a landscape painter, I fancy I see Gainsborough in every hedge and hollow tree".

Constable was open to many other artistic influences at this time. In 1785 he was introduced to Sir George Beaumont (1753-1827), an amateur artist and art collector with a family home at Dedham. Beaumont owned paintings by Claude Lorraine, the seventeenth century French classical landscape painter, admired the work of his British follower Richard Wilson (1713/14-1782) and expounded the academic doctrines of Sir Joshua Reynolds (1723-1792) the President of the Royal Academy, who was often perceived as a critic of Gainsborough's mainly self-taught and intuitive style.

Nevertheless, Constable retained an admiration for Gainsborough and the Dutch masters describing them in a lecture of 1836 as "a stay-at-home people, hence their originality". Although he lived for many years in London and for a short time at Brighton, making short visits elsewhere, Constable preferred to paint scenes near home at East Bergholt and in the surrounding Stour Valley where his family lived and worked. He was the first to concentrate on one geographical area which had so many personal associations for him. He wrote:

"But I should paint my own places best — Painting is but another word for feeling. I associate my 'careless boyhood' to all that lies on the banks of the Stour. They made me a painter (& I am gratefull)".

Many nineteenth century Suffolk artists shared Constable's love of familiar places and rarely travelled far afield. Their insularity probably has led to the scarcity of published literature about them. Frost apparently was "content to live and die amid the scenes he loved" in Ipswich. **Thomas Churchyard,** the stylistic disciple of Constable, concentrated almost entirely on scenes of Woodbridge and Melton. The Ipswich group of artists **Edward** and **Thomas Smythe, Robert Burrows,** Fred Brett Russel, **John Moore, John Duvall** and **Henry Todd** painted real or imaginary scenes of the townscape or its rural environs mainly for local patrons.

Alderman G. G. Sampson c1836 by Jabez Hare Jnr (1820-1837) Oil on canvas

John Crome (1768-1821), credited as the founder of the Norwich Society of Artists in 1803, was well acquainted with the tradition of the Dutch masters, Thomas Gainsborough and Richard Wilson. He was influential in leading his contemporaries and followers towards a school of painting which celebrated the picturesque qualities of the low-lying Norfolk landscape with its broad open skies. Suffolk artists were anxious to learn from their East Anglian neighbours. **Thomas Churchyard,** who frequently copied Crome's work and owned twenty-three paintings by Crome at his death, exhibited with the Norwich Society in 1829. **John Moore** and **Robert Burrows** painted several moonlight scenes in the manner of Crome. **Henry Bright** of Saxmundham began his art training in Norwich as an apprentice to Alfred Stannard (1806-1889) and also obtained lessons from John Berney Crome (1794-1842) and John Sell Cotman (1782-1842). **Edward Smythe** moved to Norwich to study with Frederick Ladbrooke (1810-1865) in 1840.

Ipswich — A Centre of Artistic Activity

From the 1820's, Ipswich gradually became a centre for the encouragement of artists. It had grown to be the largest and most industrialised town in the county by the 1850's with a prosperous middle class of manufacturers, merchants and tradesmen who purchased pictures for their newly built mansions and required a high standard of education for their children. The long-founded Ipswich Grammar School, accommodated at the Blackfriars Dormitory and temporary buildings in Lower Brook Street before moving to the Henley Road site in 1852, was attended by several boys who later became artists. Amongst these were Charles Keene (1823-1891) the draughtsman and illustrator, Jabez Hare (1820-1837) the "boy" portrait and animal painter, Edward Poynter (1836-1919) who became President of the Royal Academy, the first Professor at the Slade School of Art University College London in 1871 and the Director of the Royal College of Art, South Kensington from 1875 and George Thomas Rope (1846-1929) who specialised in painting horses. In 1819 Robert Burcham Clamp (1795-1875), an artist of some modest talent himself, opened a school for general education in Friars Street. His Academy moved to St Nicholas Street in 1823. It was here that the young **Edward Smythe** won first prize in 1826 for "improvement in drawing" and William Stannard, later a lithographer, was awarded one of the "principal prizes". Jabez Hare was taught by Clamp before moving to the Grammar School. Thomas Woolner (1825-1892), the Pre-Raphaelite sculptor born at Hadleigh, was apparently educated "near Ipswich up to the age of 10". Josiah Whymper (1813-1903) and his brother Ebenezer, the sons of an affluent Ipswich brewer, were born and educated in the town. Their leading wood-engraving business in London offered career opportunities in illustration to other Ipswich artists during the 1840's. These included **Samuel Read,** Charles Keene, and Jabez Hare Snr. (d.1851) the father of the young portrait painter.

It is not known how far across Suffolk the reputation of Great Barton's Henry Bunbury (1750-1811), the master of social caricature and burlesque, had spread but the art of caricature was certainly popular in Ipswich. John Smart produced some satirical drawings of Ipswich events around 1798 and **George Rowe** drew a set of *Characters of Ipswich* which were lithographically printed by Piper's Press in 1821-1822 (Ipswich Museums). **Samuel Read** produced a sketchbook containing eighty amusing portaits of Ipswich people between 1837 and 1838 and Charles Keene later became a popular illustrator for *Punch* magazine.

On 1st March 1832, the Ipswich Society of Professional and Amateur Artists was founded. Amongst its members were Robert Burcham Clamp, **Robert Burrows, Samuel Read,** the Rev Richard Cobbold (1797-1877), an amateur artist and author, Jabez Hare Jnr, Stephen Piper the local printer and publisher, and Edward FitzGerald (1809-1883). FitzGerald, a poet who later translated the *Rubaiyat of Omar Khayyam*, was a close friend of **Thomas Churchyard** (who moved with George Rowe to London in 1832) and knew Perry Nursey of Little Bealings, friend of Constable and Sir David Wilkie R.A. (1785-1841). Many years later FitzGerald was in correspondence with Thomas Woolner, he was friendly with Edwin Edwards (1823-1879) and Charles Keene often stayed with him at Woodbridge.

Perry Nursey corresponded with the Society directly. His son Claude Lorraine Richard Wilson Nursey (1820-1873), who studied under Wilkie and later lived in Ipswich, painted three large canvases of Ipswich scenes for the Town Hall in 1842 and became Headmaster of the Norwich School of Practical Art in 1854.

Using a "room under the Grammar School" before premises became available in the new Mechanics' Institute in Tavern Street in 1834, the aims of the Society were to provide an art library, copying facilities from original paintings and conversational evenings for its members.

Although an exhibition of work by Suffolk artists was proposed, the Society does not appear to have continued its activities into the 1840's. This may have been due in part to the untimely death in 1837 of Jabez Hare Jnr., who appears to have been a leading light of the Society. The Society's minute book of committee meetings does not continue after 1837, when Robert Clamp replaced Hare as Secretary.

The Mechanics' Institute, established in 1824, had appointed Edward FitzGerald's father John FitzGerald MP as its first President. It provided lectures for its subscribing members "on the principles of the arts they practice . . . and in the various branches of science and useful knowledge". Sometimes lectures were delivered on the history of painting or sculpture and John Smart Jnr. apparently provided drawing classes at the Institute until his death around 1858.

In 1850 the Suffolk Fine Arts Association, the brain-child of Thomas Baldock Ross, the Mayor of Ipswich in 1849, was established in Ipswich as an attempt to rival Norwich as an exhibiting centre. The first exhibition opened on 28th August at the New Lecture Hall, Tower Street. Most of the exhibitors were from London or Norwich, although the work of **Thomas Churchyard, Henry Bright** (one of the vice Presidents of the Association) and Henry Davy was represented. Perhaps due to lack of appreciation Churchyard and the Norwich artists did not exhibit there again, the latter possibly making a point of organising their own exhibition on the same dates as Ipswich. **Henry Bright** contributed exhibits until at least 1852. The work of the Association fizzled out in 1854.

Following the Great Exhibition of 1851, Henry Cole succeeded in establishing a national system of art education and a Central Art Training School at South Kensington. On 10th January 1859 the Ipswich School of Art, in association with South Kensington, opened at the Assembly Rooms in Northgate Street under the master William T. Griffiths. At first privately funded by donation, the School's object was "the promotion of knowledge of practical Art, and the inculcation of an improved taste among all classes of society". In addition it was hoped to extend "knowledge of the fine arts, and principles of design, as applicable to manufacturers". The School provided a rigorous programme of drawing and shading techniques from the flat and from plaster casts and taught the arts of watercolour and oil painting. Life classes were introduced in 1875 on the request of the Ipswich Art Club. Sessions were organised in the evening as well as day with separate classes for men and women. The School under Griffiths produced artists such as **Frederic George Cotman, Walter Batley** and **William Symonds** who successfully progressed to the Royal Academy and South Kensington Schools. Griffiths retired in 1906 and was replaced by **George Rushton,** a practising artist and stained glass designer. Rushton believed "A School of Art had for its main object teaching how art could be applied to Industry". He was responsible for expanding art training into the areas of book illustration, interior decoration, furniture making and metal work. Many of the young painters he personally taught at the School (until his retirement in 1929), owed a great deal to him stylistically. Amongst them were **Leonard Squirrell,** Reginald Haggar (1905-1988), Arthur Southgate (1905-1982), Albert Ribbans (1903-1966), **George Fathers,** and Elsie Haward (1882-1956).

The Ipswich Fine Art Club was founded in 1874 to "encourage art and to excite interest in its study". It's first exhibition in 1875 included works by **John Duvall,** W. T. Griffiths, **Edward Smythe, Samuel Read, Frederic George Cotman** and **William Symonds.** A new picture gallery was built for the Club in 1880 to house the annual and major loan exhibitions. It stood next to the site of the new Museum, Library and schools of Science and Art in High Street which opened in the following year. In 1887 the Club held a major exhibition of works by *Gainsborough, Constable and the Old Suffolk Artists.* This was the first time an attempt had been made to present Suffolk Artists as a distinct group and included works by Frost, Burrows, Churchyard, Bright, Read, Rowe, Bunbury, Russel, Smart, Edwin Cooper of Beccles (1785-1833), Robert Mendham of Eye (1792-1875) and Edwin Edwards.

In 1896 Christchurch Mansion, a beautiful Tudor house situated in parkland near the centre of Ipswich, opened as an archaeological museum and picture galleries. It had been given to the Borough by Felix Thornley Cobbold (1841-1909) a member of the local family of brewers, a banker and Mayor of Ipswich, who had purchased it to save it from certain demolition after the Fonnereau family's departure in 1892. Cobbold bequeathed a trust fund to finance the purchase of works of art for the Mansion. It was due to his far-sighted generosity that the Museum was able to buy pictures by Suffolk artists throughout the twentieth century, as additional Borough purchase funds were not granted until 1966. National bodies such as the National Art Collections Fund, the National Heritage Memorial Fund, the Museums & Galleries Commission (with grants administered by the V & A Museum) and the Contemporary Arts Society have consistently given grant-aid towards purchases and have allocated gifts. Locally, the Eastern Arts Association, the Ipswich Fine Art Club and the Friends of the Ipswich Museums have also contributed. Many works of art have been acquired through the generous gifts and bequests of local people and these continue to be accepted. The Ipswich Borough Museums and Galleries art collections rival those provided in many provincial cities of Britain. They display the special qualities of artistic endeavour in Suffolk which can now be appreciated as an important contribution to the map of national heritage.

Walberswick and the Influence of French Painting

The Suffolk coast often attracted artists to its shores. Edwin Edwards (1823-1879), a professional painter and etcher from 1860, lived at Dunwich. He had made the acquaintance of Fantin Latour (1836-1904) and other French artists in 1861 when he began to paint in oil. Charles Keene (1823-1891) often visited his friends Mr & Mrs Edwards while spending long summer holidays in Suffolk, and produced etchings of the harbours and jetties of Dunwich, Walberswick and Southwold.

Philip Wilson Steer, fresh from his studies at the Academie Julian and the Ecole des Beaux-Arts in Paris, began painting at Walberswick during the summer months of 1884. By 1887-88 Steer had become the leading exponent of French Impressionism in England. He was instrumental in the foundation of the New English Art Club in 1886 (originally called the Society of Anglo-French Painters) which rebelled against the academic system of the Royal Academy and presented its own exhibitions. The bond of all the founder members was their Paris training. Steer visited Walberswick every year until 1889, and was accompanied by his fellow N.E.A.C. colleague Frederick Brown (1851-1941) possibly after 1888. Many other members visited the resort such as the Irishman Walter Osborne (1859-1903), Henry Simpson of Nacton (1853-1921), Edward Stott (1859-1918), William Llewellyn (1858-1941), Allan Davidson (1873-1932) and Frank Short (1857-1945). Mark Senior (1864-1927), known to Steer and Brown through the Chelsea Art Club, and his friend the German artist Georg Sauter (1866-1937) apparently went with Steer to Walberswick in 1906. An American artist trained in Paris, Willard Leroy Metcalf (1853-1925) painted there and Charles Rennie Mackintosh (1868-1928), who had worked on the Continent, spent a period at Walberswick around 1915 in order to recuperate from the strains of his Glasgow career. The artists' "colony" which formed at Walberswick during the 1880's has been compared to the Newlyn School in Cornwall led by Stanhope A. Forbes (1857-1947) from about the same time, although it is unlikely that it had such a large community. Many Newlyn School artists had joined the N.E.A.C. in its early years but later split from the Impressionist clique because the Newlyn artists painted large exhibition pieces which required the extensive walls of the Royal Academy to show them adequately.

Some of the artists who exhibited at the Ipswich Art Club were influenced by the Newlyn movement. **The Hon Duff Tollemache** exhibited his *After the Catch* there in 1885 (Plate 29) and from at least 1903 was sending in Cornish scenes to the Royal Academy. **Walter Batley** was known to be an admirer of Stanhope Forbes's later work. Such was the popularity of Forbes in Ipswich that his *Forging the Anchor* of 1892 was one of the first purchases made for the Museum collection using the Felix Cobbold Bequest fund in 1913.

A large number of exhibitors at the N.E.A.C. were trained at the Slade. From 1876 to 1892 the Frenchman Alphonse Legros (1837-1911), as Slade Professor, insisted on impeccable drawing as the basis for all good painting. He was seen as "a prophet" to a "generation absorbed in problems of colour, lighting and atmosphere". He was replaced by Frederick Brown, who brought in Steer and Henry Tonks (1862-1937) to help him. Tonks ran the School from 1918. They made a formidable team of teachers who profoundly influenced their students. Some of the Suffolk artists who passed through this system were **Anna Airy, Leonard Squirrell, Bertram Priestman, John Millar Watt** and Effie Spring-Smith (1907-1974). **Rose Mead** studied under Frederick Brown at the Westminster School of Art before he was at the Slade. **Alfred Munnings** trained at the Norwich School of Art but

spent two short period of study at Julian's in Paris. **Harry Becker,** who went to the Royal Academy Schools at Antwerp, finished his training at the studio of Carolus Duran in Paris.

The horizons of artists working in Suffolk broadened as the new century dawned. Few of them experimented with avante-garde movements developing in the London art world, such as Cubism or Vorticism. During the First World War, isolated newcomers to Suffolk, such as Duncan Grant (1885-1978) and Vanessa Bell (1879-1961), inspired by the work of Cezanne and the French Post-Impressionists, painted colourful and lively canvases at Wissett Lodge near Halesworth. Not until 1937, when Cedric Morris (1889-1982) opened his East Anglian School of Painting and Drawing at Dedham, would a fresh and intuitive form of expression begin to seriously challenge the academic conventions maintained by the Suffolk art establishment.

N.B. Artists named in bold typeface are discussed in the biographies next to the plates.

View of Ipswich 1753 by John Clevely (fl. 1726-1777) Oil on canvas

Contents

THOMAS GAINSBOROUGH (1727-1788)

1 View near the Coast c1750-1755

Oil on canvas 81.2 x 107.7cm.

(R1941-76)

It is not known who commissioned this landscape from Gainsborough. It was sold in 1831 to Pinney who passed it to Cdr. F.V.Stopford. Ipswich Museums purchased it from his sale in London on 18th July 1941 with a grant from the National Art Collections Fund.

Thomas Gainsborough was born in Sudbury, the fifth son of a cloth merchant. After attending Sudbury Grammar School he went to London around 1740 to 1741, where he was apprenticed to Hubert Gravelot (1699-1773), a French draughtsman and engraver who was mainly responsible for introducing the Rococo style into English book illustration. By 1745 Gainsborough was working independently and studying Dutch seventeenth century landscapes in the London sale rooms. From masters such as Ruisdael, Hobbema and Wijnants he learned a great deal about pictorial composition and dramatic lighting effects. In 1748, after his father's death, Gainsborough returned to Sudbury, but moved to Ipswich by 1752 where painting was a more lucrative occupation. Here he rented a house in Foundation Street opposite the Shire Hall and made a living by painting portraits of local professional people and occasionally landed gentry. The requirements of his patrons were usually limited to a simple likeness, a head and shoulders with a dark background. Examples of these can be seen in the Ipswich Museums' collection e.g. *Samuel Kilderbee, John Sparrowe* and the *Rev. Richard Canning*. Landscapes were only required as decorative pieces for overmantels and spaces over doors. Very few art collectors at this time would have considered buying a landscape by an English painter for any other purpose. As an exception Gainsborough had been commissioned by the Rector of Hadleigh to paint a view of Hadleigh church around 1748 to 1750 as an accurate record of the building. (This is now at Gainsborough's House, Sudbury).

View near the Coast displays Gainsborough's early use of Dutch pictorial structure, serpentine composition derived from the Rococo and a tight handling of warm tones of paint. Possibly inspired by Cuyp, whose work was becoming popular amongst collectors, Gainsborough produced an artificial landscape peopled with rustic figures and cows.

He often worked in his studio from models he had made of animals and figures and mock scenes created from natural materials, cork, coal and glass. In later life, especially after his move to London in 1774, his "fancy" landscape paintings had become fashionable as valid works of art in their own right. By this time his compositions were often based on rustic cottage scenes with groups of children and animals and his brushwork had become loose and feathery. The pair of landscapes *Cottage Door with Girl and Pigs* and *Crossing the Ford*, which were painted around 1786 for the 6th Earl of Dysart of Helmingham Hall in Suffolk, are excellent examples of Gainsborough's late style. They were acquired by the Ipswich Museums in 1982.

Bibliography:

Hayes, J., *Thomas Gainsborough* (Exh. cat. Tate Gallery London, 1980).

Hayes, J., *The Landscape Paintings of Thomas Gainsborough* Vols I & II (London, 1982) pp.82-83.

Waterhouse, E., *Gainsborough* (London, 1958).

THOMAS GAINSBOROUGH (1727-1788)

2a Mrs Bedingfield and her Daughter 1760s

Oil on canvas 128.3 x 102.8cm. (R1973-106)

This was passed by Mrs Bedingfield's brother Captain Robert Blake to his daughter and down through the Crowther-Beynon family to Mrs R. M. Goode. It was purchased by the Ipswich Museums in 1973 with grants from the government fund administered by the Victoria & Albert Museum, and the National Art Collections Fund.

Very little is known about the sitter Mrs Bedingfield who probably would have lived in Bath when this was painted.

2b William Wollaston c1759

Oil on canvas 127.5 x 100.3cm. (R1946-29)

Commisioned by the sitter, this portrait remained in the possession of the Wollaston family until 1888, when it was sold into private hands. It was purchased for the Ipswich Museums at Christie's sale of the E.J. Wythes collection on 1st March 1946.

William Wollaston (1730-1797) of Finborough Hall near Stowmarket was M.P. for Ipswich in 1768, 1774 and 1780 and was appointed Colonel of the East Suffolk Militia in 1769. He is shown holding a one-keyed boxwood flute. The sheet of music open on his lap is not playable.

During his Ipswich period, Gainsborough made a number of life-long friendships. Amongst these were Samuel Kilderbee (1725-1813) an attorney who was Town Clerk for a time, Joshua Kirby (1716-1774) son of the author of *The Suffolk Traveller*, a topographer, house and coach painter and expert in the art of perspective, and Philip Thicknesse (1719-1792) Lieutenant-Governor of Landguard Fort off the Felixstowe coast. Thicknesse, who owned a winter residence in Bath, may have been partly responsible for persuading Gainsborough to move to the spa in 1759 where he could introduce him to new circles of patrons. The portrait of Wollaston was painted shortly before their departure. An amateur flautist, Wollaston could have met Gainsborough through the Ipswich Musical Club which ran fortnightly concerts. Gainsborough was an enthusiasic musician himself and played several keyboard and stringed instruments, especially the viol da gamba. The pose of the sitter was influenced possibly by the statue of *George Frederick Handel* by Louis Francois Roubiliac (b.1705?-1762) of 1738 (Victoria & Albert Museum, London) and the portrait of *Captain Coram* by Willian Hogarth (1697-1764) of 1740 (Thomas Coram Foundation for Children, London). It is a dynamic portrait with Rococo rhythms swirling in alternating directions. Reflected light dances across the figure of Wollaston in his plush velvet waistcoat and silk-lined jacket gleaming with gold braid. Gainsborough has caught the dignity and informality of the sitter, who pauses from playing his flute as his attention is diverted for a moment.

During his early years in Bath, Gainsborough saw many outstanding collections of old masters in local country houses. He was excited by Ruben's landscapes and a number of full-length portraits by Van Dyck which greatly influenced his style. His portraits of the 1760's reveal a technical brilliance far beyond his early Suffolk work. His delight in details of costume, the simplicity of pose and the subtlety of colour absorbed from a knowledge of Van Dyck's portraits, can be clearly observed in *Mrs Bedingfield and her Daughter.*

Bibliography:

Hayes, J., *Gainsborough* (London, 1974)

Einberg, E., ed., *Manners & Morals: Hogarth and British Painting 1700-1760* (Exh. cat. Tate Gallery London, 1987). See also under Plate 1.

GEORGE FROST (1745-1821)

3   Portraits of a Horse and Ostler — Blue Coach Office Ipswich c1780-1813

Ink and watercolour 22.6 x 27.8cm.

Signed (with title) on mount, bottom right: *Frost*

(R1944-149)

This was purchased from Gooden & Fox Ltd, London in 1944. Its previous source is unkown.

The son of a builder, George Frost was born at Ousden and brought up at Barrow in Suffolk. He arrived in Ipswich as a young man to take up the position of clerk in the Blue Coach Office in Upper Brook Street. Here he directed the arrival and departure of the London coaches and ensured they were kept with their horses overnight at the Coach and Horses Inn.

This watercoloured drawing in fluid ink shows a stableman from the inn preparing a horse for its journey. The coach started for London at 7.00am and so Frost would have been up at dawn to capture the luminous pink light pervading this scene. After the morning's business had been completed, Frost's wife managed the office, enabling Frost to go out on sketching expeditions for the rest of the day. In his delicate watercolours, often done on the spot, he immortalised the changing topography of the Cornhill, Ipswich. He recorded the destruction of the Shambles in 1794, the erection and demolition of the Rotunda followed by the building of the first Ipswich Corn Exchange on that site in 1810 and the demolition of the Market Cross in 1812. He was often at the bustling Common Quay sketching the horse-drawn wagons loaded with corn, men stacking barrels or cranes shifting goods on to ships. He drew the old Bourne and Stoke bridges, the windmills at Stoke and the sandy tracks on the shores of the River Orwell. His favourite haunts outside the town appear to have been Bramford, Freston, Trimley, Orford and the area around Butley Abbey. An intelligent, well-read and modest man he was highly regarded by local art connoisseurs who welcomed him into their homes. In 1813 Frost retired from the Coach Office and moved to a house on the Common Quay. His prolific output of scenes and sketches is well represented in the Ipswich Borough Museums collection.

Bibliography:

Bennet t, C., *The River Orwell: Artists' Views of Ipswich and its Waterfront over Two Centuries* (Ipswich, 1988).
Brown, F., *Frost's Drawings of Ipswich and Sketches in Suffolk* (Ipswich, 1895).
Clarke, G.R., *The History & Description of Ipswich* (London 1830).
Hayes, J., *The Drawings of George Frost (1745-1821)* MASTER DRAWINGS (November, 1966) pp. 163-168.

References:

SC: 22.2.1859, Suffolk Worthies and Persons of Note in East Anglia: No 46 — George Frost.
EADT: 4.11.1933, Worthies of Ipswich No XVIII — George Frost of Happy Memory.

GEORGE FROST (1745-1821)

4 **'Ladies in the Mall'** c1820

Oil on canvas 93.5 x 119cm.

(R1985-78)

Purchased by William Brown of Ipswich from a sale of the artist's effects in 1821, this painting remained in the possession of the Brown family until 1985. Ipswich Museums purchased it from D. E. Brown, with financial assistance from one of his relatives.

It is believed that Frost moved to Ipswich a few years after **Thomas Gainsborough** had left the town. An 1814 reproduction of a drawing by Frost dated 1780 shows that he was a practising artist by this time. In 1797, **John Constable** had learned about Frost's sketching expeditions in Gainsborough's footsteps on the banks of the Orwell, and that he was known as a drawing master. Frost's enthusiasm for Gainsborough's drawings and the emulation of his sketching style may have influenced the young Constable who went on sketching trips with him and with whom he was thought to be " on intimate terms of friendship". Frost also appears to have been one of the first to express an admiration for Constable's work. Frost built up a valuable collection of drawings and paintings by Gainsborough, which he regularly copied. In 1820 Thomas Green described his drawings "principally with black chalk and lead pencil" remarking "how keen a relish he has imbibed the genius and spirit of his adopted master". After a visit to the artist's studio on October 16th in the same year, Green wrote in his diary:

"Called on Frost copying his large Gainsbrough, the Mall and St James's Park. An airy, flimsy production, evincing much dexterity of hand and skill in colouring, but still no picture. He has manifestly proved Frost's ruin as an artist". Frost had written to Constable in London on 6th September 1807 about the "Scene on the Park" he intended to buy, admitting that it bore "no comparison in beauty or value to his usual landskips — but it is Gainsbro . . . . there is beautiful pencilling".

Gainsborough had painted *The Mall in St James's Park* in 1783 for George III, although it did not enter the Royal Collections and remained unsold in his studio when he died. According to William Jackson, a contemporary of Gainsborough, "all the female figures in his Park-scene Gainsborough drew from a doll of his own creation". Other contemporaries called it "all a flutter, like a lady's fan" and "to the manner of Watteau".

Gainsborough's *"Mall"* later passed to a London dealer who sold it to Mr Sparrow of Ipswich. Frost, who had seen the painting at Gainsborough's sale of effects in London in 1788 or 1789, bought it from Sparrow after 1807. Frost's copy of *"The Mall"* was believed to have been his last major work before he died in 1821. The original version by Gainsborough, after passing through several private hands after Frost's death, entered the Frick Collection, New York in 1916.

Bibliography:
See No 3 and
Beckett, R.B., *John Constable's Correspondence* Vol II (Suffolk, 1964)
Whitley, W.T., *Thomas Gainsborough* (London, 1915)

DANIEL COOPER (1749-1822)

5 'Courtship' 1777

Oil on canvas 76.3 x 63.7cm. (R1972-13)

This picture remained in the possession of the Clutten family until it was presented to Ipswich Museums in 1792.

The subjects for this double portrait are James Clutten (1755-1837) and Alicia Cooper (1755-1808) both of Fressingfield, who were married at Fressingfield Church (seen on the right) on 22nd June 1779. Alicia Cooper was the artist's sister.

Daniel Cooper was born at Fressingfield, Suffolk, the son of Daniel Cooper Snr (1719-1781), a prosperous Fressingfield landowner and his wife Elizabeth. Young Daniel became an Ensign in the Suffolk Fencibles but was persuaded by his wife Martha Hockley, to resign his commission in order to study for the artist's profession. At first he was taught drawing and sculpture by a minor artist called Martineau. According to Desmond Taylor, he may also have received advice from Sir Joshua Reynolds (1723-1792) the President of the Royal Academy who was, no doubt, besieged by aspiring young portrait painters for guidance from all over the country. He moved with his wife to Nottingham, where he became a drawing master at a local school, and where she opened a School for Young Ladies. Taylor says that Cooper was living at 2 Eastgate Street, Bury St Edmunds from 1779, the year of his marriage at St James's Church in Bury. (The date of marriage stated in the Parish Register as 1779 contradicts Taylor's date of 1769). The Bury Rate Books indicate that Cooper was living at the Eastgate Street address in Bury from 1791 to 1817. Therefore it appears more likely that the Coopers would have moved to Nottingham after their marriage in 1779 and returned to Suffolk by 1791, having tragically lost seven children in infancy during their twelve years in the north of England.

No 2 Eastgate Street was next door to the King Edward VI Grammar School which had a very high reputation at this time. Cooper was employed at the School as a drawing master.

During the eighteenth century, Bury St Edmunds had become well established as a social, administrative and cultural centre in West Suffolk. Although it was not the county town, it was the venue for the county law courts and was well populated with gentry, professional people and wealthy tradesmen. It was also conveniently near Newmarket, the fashionable horse racing town. Daniel Cooper would have been well placed for receiving portrait commissions in such a thriving environment.

Three more children were born: Edwin, Frances and Anne. Edwin Cooper (1785-1833) showed an early talent for drawing and later became a professional animal and sporting painter. Anne, his sister, also was an artist. After Martha Cooper died in 1814, Daniel remarried and had at least one more child.

When Daniel Cooper's will was proved at Norwich in 1822 he was described as being of Norwich and formerly of Tivetshall St Mary. According to Taylor, he had retired to his farm called 'Finches' at Fressingfield. It is possible that he had inherited several properties from his father.

Only one other painting by Daniel Cooper is known: a portrait miniature of his son Edwin.

Bibliography:
Clutton, W.D., *Genealogy & Family History of William Clutten (1675-1732) of Fressingfield, Suffolk, England and his Descendents* (MS Suffolk Record Office)
Fiske, J., ed., *The Oakes Diaries Vol I: Business, Politics and the Family in Bury St Edmunds 1778-1806* (Suffolk, 1990)
Taylor, D., *Edwin Cooper of Beccles (1785-1833)* (Leigh-on-Sea, 1980)
References:
EADT: 21.5.1932 Article on Daniel and Edwin Cooper and the portrait 'Courtship'

JOHN CONSTABLE (1776-1837)

6   Golding Constable's Flower Garden 1815

Oil on canvas 33 x 50.8cm.

(R1955-96.1)

This picture, and its pair Plate 7, were disposed of by the artist's descendants. They were sold at Christie's on 11th July 1887 and passed through the hands of several auctioneers, dealers and private owners. Ernest Cook of Bath bequeathed them to the Ipswich Museums through the National Art Collections Fund.

The garden scenes, reproduced here and on the next page, were painted probably from an upstairs window or from the roof of East Bergholt House, the home of Constable's parents.

John Constable was born at East Bergholt, the second son of Anne Watts and Golding Constable, described in his day as a "man of fortune and a miller, has a very elegant house in the street and lives in the style of a country squire". Golding Constable also shipped grain from Mistley, on the River Stour, and imported coal which was transported in his own barges built at Flatford where he owned the Mill.

In 1802 Constable bought a studio near his parents house in East Bergholt where he worked during the summer months every year. On 29th May, 1802 he wrote to his friend John Dunthorne:

"For these two years past I have been running after pictures and seeking the truth at second hand. . . . . . I shall shortly return to Bergholt where I shall make some laborious studies from nature — and I shall endeavour to get a pure and unaffected representation of the scenes that may employ me with respect to colour particularly and anything else . . . . .".

Between 1802 and 1812 Constable's laborious small oil sketches of the local scenery developed into brilliant and lively expressions of what he personally felt about it. These sketches, however, were intended as preparatory ideas for larger paintings completed in his studio and not as finished pictures in themselves.

In 1814 he made two pencil drawings similar to the *'Garden'* scenes at the rear of East Bergholt House, both called *View over the Constable Farm* (Victoria & Albert Museum). It is possible that the paintings were, unusually, completed on the spot as there is no other evidence of preliminary work and the detail has been meticulously handled. Rosenthal suggests that the *'Kitchen Garden'* was painted in the morning and the *'Flower Garden'* in the evening during August 1815. One of the pencil drawings, inscribed with the date "22 Sepr 1814", shows a half ploughed field.

These paintings are celebrations of the agricultural landscape at its peak, with an underlying theme of the relationships between working people, the fields and the village. Harvesting, threshing and milling are observed as serving the needs of the honest villagers who proudly cultivate their own garden plots.

Bibliography:
Rosenthal, M., *Constable, the Painter and His Landscape* (New Haven London, 1983)
References:
Beckett, R.B., *John Constable's Correspondence* Vol II (Suffolk, 1964) pp.31-32

JOHN CONSTABLE (1776-1837)

7   **Golding Constable's Kitchen Garden** 1815

Oil on canvas 33 x 50.8cm.

(R1955-96.2)

See Plate 6.

It was John Constable's introduction in 1795 to Sir George Beaumont, the art connoisseur (see Introduction, p.iv) which set Constable's mind on becoming an artist. He paticularly admired Beaumont's *Landscape with Hagar and the Angel* by Claude Lorraine. In 1796 Constable met the artist J.T. Smith and eagerly corresponded with him for artistic advice and encouragement. At this time Constable was only an amateur, copying and going out sketching with John Dunthorne, the local plumber, glazier and occasional sign painter. (John Dunthorne Jnr (1798-1832) later became Constable's studio assistant). Constable could have met **George Frost** soon after 1797. In 1799 he entered the Royal Academy Schools as a probationer and fully enrolled as a student in 1800.

In 1806 Constable spent two months in the Lakes. He was unenthusiastic about the place saying later that "the solitude of the mountains oppressed his spirits". His friend and biographer C.R. Leslie explained further:

"His nature was particularly social and could not feel satisfied with scenery, however grand in itself, that did not abound in human associations. He required villages, churches, farmhouses and cottages; and I believe it was as much from natural temperament as from early impressions that his first love, in landscape, was also his latest love".

During the early years of the new century, Constable painted several landscapes and portraits for local people but could not yet earn his living. The private income he received after his father's death in 1816 enabled him to continue his career and marry Maria Bicknell. They were married by his friend John Fisher, nephew of the Bishop of Salisbury, and spent part of their honeymoon at Fisher's vicarage at Osmington in Dorset. Constable rarely sketched places outside East Anglia unless they were visited for personal reasons. He painted Osmington and Salisbury as well as Hampstead and Brighton, where he set up new homes with Maria for the sake of her health.

The international acclaim, which Constable now receives is a twentieth century phenomenon. Although his paintings shown in Paris in 1821 influenced some contemporary French landscape artists, he only received measured recognition in England during his life-time. The persistence of his family and friends after his death in 1837 brought about a steady growth in interest. Collectors like **Thomas Churchyard** and Edward FitzGerald probably played their part. It was not until 1888, when Isobel Constable gave a large collection of Constable's work to the Victoria & Albert Museum, that a new public, aware of French Impressionism, could appreciate the brilliance and original vision of Constable's oil sketches.

Bibliography:
See Plate 6
Reynolds, G., *Constable: The Natural Painter* (London, 1965)

References:
Leslie, C.R., *Memoirs of the Life of John Constable* (London, 1951) pp. 18-19

THOMAS CHURCHYARD (1798-1865)

8 Melton Quay

Oil on panel 20.2 x 30.5cm.

Inscribed on reverse, top right: *Harriet Churchyard*
TC

(R1971-108)

This picture was given by the artist to a Mr Hart who passed it to Vincent Redstone, history master at Woodbridge School. He bequeathed it to his daughters Elsie and Lilian. It was presented by Miss E. Restone to the Ipswich Museums in 1971.

This scene shows Wilford Bridge over the River Deben on the far left, with Melton Quay hidden behind the central buildings.

Thomas Churchyard was the only son of a Melton butcher and grazier, and the first of a long line of Suffolk yeomen and tradesmen to take up a profession. Following his education at Dedham Grammar School, Churchyard was articled to Robert Crabtree, a Halesworth solicitor, between 1816 and 1820 with a final year in London in 1821. He commenced practice as a lawyer in Woodbridge from 1822, where he became highly regarded as a conscientious and brilliant man who often saved lost causes.

Churchyard also dreamed of becoming a professional landscape painter and throughout his life he eagerly collected and copied paintings by his favourite artist John Crome of Norwich (1768-1821). He also owned works by **Thomas Gainsborough** and **George Frost** of Suffolk, and other British artists in search of the picturesque such as Richard Wilson and George Morland. The second major influence on his own work after Crome was **John Constable,** whose paintings found a treasured place in the Churchyard collection.

In 1829 Churchyard exhibited at the Norwich Society of Artists exhibition and was duly elected an honorary member. In 1830 he exhibited at the Society of British Artists in Suffolk Street and in the following year at the Royal Academy. In 1832 he made an unsuccessful attempt to establish himself as a professional artist in London, sharing a studio with his Woodbridge friend the artist **George James Rowe** at 7, Upper Stamford Street. He returned to his wife, growing young family and legal career in Suffolk in 1833.

During the 1840's Churchyard's often over ambitious art collecting enterprises encouraged his close Woodbridge friends the poets Edward Fitzgerald (1809-1883) and Bernard Barton (1784-1849) to follow similar pursuits. Churchyard's later years were troubled by increasing financial difficulties. His desire to protect some bequest of future value for his seven daughters led him to inscribe on the reverse side of each of his own mostly unsigned and undated pictures their individual names: Ellen, Emma, Laura, Anna, Bessie, Harriet and Kate. It was only through the elderly Harriet's efforts, later sales of her effects and twentieth century public exhibitions that Thomas Churchyard's artistic achievement could receive the recognition it enjoys today.

Bibliography: See Plate 9.

THOMAS CHURCHYARD (1798-1865)

9   Ploughing

Oil on pine panel 13.7 x 17.9cm.

(R1913-2.2)

This was one of eighty works by Churchyard in the collection of John Wrinch, a Woodbridge friend of Churchyard's daughters, who died in 1906. They were sold by his widow to the Ipswich Borough Museums in 1913.

Thomas Churchyard loved to paint outdoors almost daily making small oil and watercolour sketches of the familiar scenes around Melton and Woodbridge. He rarely painted outside the locality and often took his artistic children with him on painting excursions. Churchyard became a master of capturing the exact time of day or the effects of changing weather in a fleeting moment.

His style from the 1830's owed a great deal to the work of John Constable. It is not known if the two artists actually met although they might well have done so. Churchyard knew Constable's Woodbridge patron the solicitor James Pulham as well as his friend Perry Nursey of Little Bealings. Constable's occasional visits to the Woodbridge area are well recorded in his dated sketches and correspondence.

Whereas Constable's outdoor sketches were intended as preparatory records which were then synthesised over a period of time into paintings completed in his studio, Churchyard saw his own sketches as finished works in themselves.

In a letter of 29 April 1847, Bernard Barton wrote of Churchyard:

"He will dash you off slight and careless sketches by the dozen, or score, but for touching and re-touching, or finishing, that is quite another affair, and has to wait, if even it be done at all".

In this tiny ploughing scene near the banks of the river Deben, Churchyard using a limited palette, lightly worked his brush over the surface leaving the natural colour and grains of the wooden panel to show through. In doing so he produced a simple and harmonious composition of man and nature working as one under a glorious autumn sky.

Bibliography:
Thomas, D., *Thomas Churchyard of Woodbridge* (Kent, 1966)
Morfey, W., *Painting the Day: Thomas Churchyard of Woodbridge* (Suffolk, 1986)

GEORGE JAMES ROWE (1807-1883)

10   The River Deben below Waldringfield 1830

Oil on panel 14.8 x 22.8cm.

Contemporary label on reverse inscribed: *River Deben*

1830   G. J Rowe

(R1954-72)

This picture was purchased from Garrod Turner's saleroom Ipswich by Ipswich Museums in 1954. It's previous source is inknown.

George James Rowe was the son of an ex-army surgeon practising at Well Street, Woodbridge after 1815. Around 1825, **Thomas Churchyard** moved to 29 Well Street and it could have been as neighbours, if not earlier, that the two aspiring artists began their life-long friendship. The earliest known drawings by a George Rowe are the *Characters of Ipswich* (Ipswich Museums), lithographically printed between 1821 and 1822 by Stephen Piper of Ipswich. They include studies of celebrated professional and tradespeople of the town and would have been completed when Rowe was only 14. It is not certain that the Rowe who drew these *'Characters'* was the same person as the landscape painter from Woodbridge, although there is little reason to doubt of the connection. A number of other collaborations between Rowe and Piper in print such as the *Remains of St George's Chapel, Ipswich* (Suffolk Record Office) are fairly rudimentary and perhaps youthful achievements.

In 1830 Rowe exhibited a *Study from Nature* at the Norwich Society of Artists exhibition and had a work accepted by the Royal Academy. In 1831 a Woodbridge auctioneer advertised the sale of "Prints, Drawings, Paintings, and Grease Drawings of Mr George Rowe, Drawing Master, who is leaving the town". Rowe left Woodbridge with Churchyard in 1832 to set up as professional artists in London, where they shared a studio at 7, Upper Stamford Street. Churchyard returned to Suffolk in 1833 and Rowe kept his Woodbridge address until 1844. After then, he began to send work to the RA from 16 Buckingham Street, Fitzroy Square and, for the last time, from 21 Carburton Street in 1854. He also exhibited at the British Institution and the Society of British Artists, Suffolk Street.

Rowe would have had access to original works by **John Constable** and John Crome through the collections of his friend Churchyard. The small oil sketch reproduced here, probably done on the spot, is a delightfully naive and brave attempt to combine the new painterly formulae of Constable's oil sketches with John Crome's muted colouring and lighting effects.

His obituary in the Ipswich Journal described him as a painter "who has attained a high degree of excellence in his art . . . . . . Mr Rowe was for some years resident in Woodbridge, where he was well known and respected, and had many pupils and friends, amongst them being Mr. J.B. Hart". (J. Brook Hart was a founder member of the Ipswich Fine Art Club in 1874 and a friend of the Churchyard family).

In 1884 Rowe's sister, having emigrated to America, donated almost a thousand of his sketches, watercolours and prints to the Davenport Public Museum, Iowa, where they remain today.

Bibliography:

Morfey, W.M., *Painting the Day: Thomas Churchyard of Woodbridge* (Suffolk, 1986)

References:

IJ: 17.2.1883 Obituary for G. Rowe

HENRY BRIGHT (1810-1873)

11 Landscape with Windmill 1841

Oil on canvas 38.7 x 53.3cm.

Signed and dated, bottom left: *H. Bright 1841.*

(R1921-2)

This picture was purchased by Ipswich Museums from Gooden & Fox Ltd of London in 1921. Its previous source is unknown.

Henry Bright was the son of the Saxmundham clockmaker Jerome Bright (1770-1846) and Susannah Denney of Alburgh, Norfolk. It is believed that Henry was born at the family home and business premises in Saxmundham High Street. There is conflicting evidence about his exact date of birth.

Bright attended a "School for Young Gentlemen in North Entrance Saxmundham" run by Owen Haxell, possibly in the company of Thomas Thurlow (1813-1899), who later became a sculptor. At an early age, Bright moved to Woodbridge as a chemist's apprentice. His parents transferred him to a Norwich chemist, but Bright's artistic hopes were fulfilled when his indentures passed to the artist Alfred Stannard (1806-1889) of Norwich. Apparently, he also took lessons from John Berney Crome (1794-1842), and John Sell Cotman (1782-1842) who were leading members of the Norwich Society of Artists. Bright developed life-long friendships from this period with the amateur artists Thomas Lound (1802-1861), Robert Leman (1799-1863) and William Philip Barnes Freeman (1813-1897). In 1833 Bright returned to Saxmundham to marry Eliza Brightley at the Parish Church and in 1836 they moved to Paddington, London where they lived at various addresses. Bright exhibited mainly watercolours at first at the British institution and the Society of British Artists in Suffolk Street. Later, he exhibited oils at the Royal Hibernian Academy in Dublin in 1843 and at the Royal Academy from 1845. In 1839 he became a member of the New Society of Painters in Watercolours, until his resignation in 1845. Bright was a member of the Graphic Society of Painters and Engravers during the 1850's. He spent a portion of every year on sketching tours of the British Isles and the Continent. During the 1840's and 1850's he visited Holland, France, Germany and Prussia. It was on one of his continental trips that he met J.M.W. Turner (1775-1851), a future friend.

In London, Bright's work was a financial success and he became a celebrated art teacher of the upper classes and aristocracy. One of his patrons was Sir Robert Peel, a collector of Dutch and Flemish paintings, whose daughter was his pupil.

From 1848 he exhibited with the Norfolk & Norwich Association for the Promotion of Fine Arts and was one of the Vice Presidents for the Suffolk Association of Fine Arts in Ipswich between 1850 and 1852. In 1858, ill health led to a move to his brother's house at Park Lodge, Saxmundham. After further moves, he was in Ipswich by 1868, and by 1870 he was living at 22 Anglesea Road with his niece, where he continued to paint until his death in 1873. He was buried at Ipswich Cemetery. His obituary in the *Suffolk Chronicle* of 27th September 1873 noted that "For splendid sky effects Bright was second only to Turner. In some of his pictures the sky is surcharged with heavy clouds, and the portrayal of rain is singularly powerful . . . . His crayon drawings were almost unequalled, and in all respects he may be said to have been a worthy associate in art with Gainsborough and Constable, of whom Suffolk people may well be proud."

Bright had several Suffolk patrons. No fewer than twenty-five of his pictures from local lenders were exhibited in the *Loan Exhibition of works by Gainsborough, Constable & Old Suffolk Artists* at the Art Gallery Ipswich in 1887.

Bibliography:
Allthorpe-Guyton, M., *Henry Bright 1810-1873: Paintings & Drawings in Norwich Castle Museum (Norfolk, 1986)*

EDWARD ROBERT SMYTHE (1810-1899)

12 **'Awaiting the Fishing Fleet'** c1855?

Oil on canvas 40.7 x 56cm.

Signed, bottom left: *E R Smythe.*

(R1931-28.21)

This was collected by Robert Allen of Ipswich (1848-1920) and bequeathed by his widow Mrs Rosalie Allen to the Ipswich Museums in 1931.

Edward Robert Smythe was born in Berners Street, Ipswich in 1810 the son of James Smythe, an accountant with Bacon's Bank and his wife Sara Harriet. (The name Smith was probably changed to Smythe later in the century). His younger brother was the artist **Thomas Smythe.** Edward Smythe attended Robert Burcham Clamp's school which had opened in Friars Street in 1819 before moving to St Nicholas Street in 1823. In July 1826 the first prize for "improvement in drawing" went to Master Edward Smythe, then aged sixteen. Although he was attracted to the possibility of a military career, his association with other Ipswich artists led him to take up painting professionally. In Ipswich he knew Fred Brett Russel, Walter Hagreen, **Robert Burrows** and **Sam Read,** who visited his studio at the Old Shire Hall, Foundation Street. It is reasonable to suppose that the charicature Read drew of an "E. Smith" between 1837 and 1838 was the artist Edward Smythe.

In 1840 Smythe went to Norwich to study with the second generation of Norwich School artists. He formed a friendship with Frederick Ladbrooke (1810-1865), one of three artistic sons of Robert Ladbrooke (1769-1842). He is believed to have become friendly with Claude Lorraine Nursey (1820-1873) in Norwich (see Introduction p.vi).

Smythe returned to Ipswich, but after 1850 he moved to Bury St. Edmunds. He was in Ipswich again from 1886 until his death.

During his career, Smythe exhibited at the Royal Academy, the British Institution and the Society of British Artists. He was a loyal exhibitor with the Ipswich Art Club from 1875 to 1898.

His work reveals an awareness of the Dutch masters. There is a remarkable similarity between the beach scene illustrated here and *A View on a Seashore, with Fishwives Offering Fish to a Horseman* by Philips Wouvermans, which was in Sir Robert Peel's collection of Dutch and Flemish masters between 1824 and 1871, (the year the National Gallery acquired the collection from Peel). It is unlikely that Smythe would have painted his scene as late as 1871 when the Wouvermans first became available to the public gaze. Smythe's tight handling of paint is characteristic of his earlier style and it is just possible that this was the work he exhibited at the Royal Academy in 1855 entitled *Beach Scene.* **Henry Bright** had seen Peel's collection at Drayton Manor, Staffordshire by 1850. It is remotely possible that Smythe had access to it by some association with Bright.

Bibliography:
Bethell, D., *The Smythes of Ipswich* (Exh. Cat. The Debenham Gallery, 1989).

References:
EADT: 6.7.1899 Obituary; EADT: 10.7.1899 News of Funeral.
EADT: 5.1936, *Worthies of Ipswich* No 41 E. R. Smythe.

EDWARD ROBERT SMYTHE (1810-1899)

13   'The Colne Valley Viaduct' 1850

Oil on canvas 92 x 137.5cm.

(R1939-194)

This painting appeared at the Royal Academy in 1850 entitled "View of the Colne Valley at Chappel, Essex, through which passes the railway to Sudbury". It was acquired by Peter Schuyler Bruff (1812-1900), of Handford Lodge, Ipswich "the Brunel of the Eastern Counties" and the engineer who designed and built the viaduct shown in the painting. It was bequeathed to Ipswich Borough Council in 1900 (with plate 25), and later passed to the Museums.

The Stour Valley railway line from Marks Tey to Sudbury was approved by Parliament in 1846. The building of the viaduct, probably Bruff's most ambitious project, was to enable the product of "ploughshare and loom to reach the greatest market in the world". Using locally-made bricks from Mount Bures clay, the viaduct was built between 1847 and 1849, rising 80 feet above the River Colne, totalling 1,066 feet in length with thirty-two arches. It carried the Sudbury line over the Colne Valley at Chappel, and now joins the parishes of Wakes Colne and Chappel over the A604.

This picture (wrongly attributed to Fred Brett Russel for many years), was Edward Smythe's first exhibit at the Royal Academy in 1850. It is an early attempt at painting in the 'grand manner' after his training period at Norwich. The dramatic lighting and treatment of rustic scenery could have been derived from the work of artists such as George Vincent (1796-1832), James Stark (1794-1859) and the later Ladbrookes (see Plate 12). Smythe's inclusion of the Italian-styled peasants, with their pack-horse in the foreground, and his use of the compositional formulae of Claude Lorraine (who painted the countryside around Rome in the seventeenth century), has implied a link between Bruff's monumental viaduct, with its Romanesque arches, and actual Roman architecture of classical antiquity.

Bibliography:
See 12 & 14
Moffat, H., *East Anglia's First Railways* (Suffolk, 1987)

EDWARD ROBERT SMYTHE (1810-1899)

14 Winter

Oil on canvas 61.3 x 91.6cm.

Signed, bottom left: *E R Smythe*

(R1932-42)

This was presented to the Ipswich Museums by the executors of Alderman John Henry Grimwade in 1932.

Edward Smythe's work was well patronised by Ipswich and Norwich art collectors as well as the nobility.

The 7th Earl of Cardigan commissioned him to paint a large canvas representing the famous *Charge of Balaclava*. He and other surviving officers gave him many sittings and their horses were also sent down from London in order to ensure that every detail was reproduced faithfully.

In 1846 Smythe painted the backdrop to the Feline Case in the Ipswich Museum, representing a mountain and desert scene in Africa. This was paid for by the Marquis of Bristol. Smythe's work was keenly collected in Ipswich by Robert Allen and Alfred Stearn. Thomas Neale Fonnereau, the owner of Christchurch Mansion, also owned one or two pictures by him.

Smythe's main influences were **Thomas Gainsborough, John Constable,** George Morland (1763-1804), John Crome (1768-1821) and Edwin Landseer (1802-1873). He specialised in sentimental landscapes and interiors of country life and incorporated children (often his own) with horses, ponies and dogs and other animals into his scenes.

He often painted the blacksmith at work in the smithy, a subject Landseer had popularised in his *Shoeing* of 1844 (Tate Gallery). Landseer's touching scenes of people in domestic interiors with their pets and portraits of horses and dogs with humanised expressions were not only collected by the Royal Family and prominent families of the nobility but they were also widely published in the form of engravings. Smythe's genre paintings appealed to the same taste amongst the art collectors of his era.

Smythe rarely dated his pictures and the dating process can only be cautiously attempted by detecting a stylistic progression. Topographically accurate views of identifiable places are also uncommon, although they do exist. Like those of his brother **Thomas Smythe**, many of Edward Smythe's scenes were imaginary and based on an idyllic view of rural life, using a formula of traditional landscape compositions inhabited by peasants in mid-Victorian costume.

Bibliography:
See Plate 12
Johnson, E.D.H., *Painting of the British Social Scene from Hogarth to Sickert* (London, 1986)

ROBERT BURROWS (1810-1883)

15 **Foxhall Road, Ipswich** 1867

Oil on canvas 30.6 x 41cm.

Signed and dated, bottom left: *Robert Burrows 1867*

(R1936-442)

This was purchased at auction at the Arcade Hall, Ipswich by Ipswich Museums in 1936. The label on the reverse of the frame is inscribed with the name "G. H. Poole (or Potter?), Neale Street", who could have been a previous owner.

Born in Ipswich, Robert Burrows was the eldest son of Robert Burrows Snr, a silversmith of Old Cattle Market and his wife Elizabeth Cordy. Young Robert carried on the family business from Silent Street and in White's 1855 Directory he is listed as "silversmith, pawnbroker, insurance agent for London Assurance Company, music teacher and artist."

In 1832 he became a member of the Ipswich Society of Professional and Amateur Artists, alongside **Samuel Read,** Robert Burcham Clamp and Jabez Hare Jnr. He had artistic friends outside the Society such as **Edward Robert Smythe** who was probably the main influence on his work. In 1835 Burrows married Harriet Batterbee Bowman, the daughter of an Ipswich brewer. Edward Smythe drew a portrait of the couple which (going by the costumes worn) would have been produced around 1855. As Smythe signed it, "E. Smythe of Bury St. Edmunds" it certainly dates to after 1850 when he arrived in Bury. This is now in the Suffolk Record Office.

On 1st November 1847 he was elected an Ipswich town councillor, as a Liberal for the Bridge Ward. He was re-elected in 1850 and 1853 but defeated in 1856. It is thought that he developed an interest in photography around 1857 as a result of this change in his circumstances.

Burrows was responsible for the earliest known photographic records of Ipswich scenes and people. The photographic processes he used date some of his work to around 1857 to 1860. The photographs which he took in his studio often look artifically posed. This was probably due to Burrow's desire for an artistic arrangement and the long exposure period required to take the shot.

After Burrows's wife died in 1869 he took up painting full time. In a letter to a Mr William Davy, a collector of his pictures, he wrote: "I have sold off and taken good lodgings, keeping my rooms as before for painting in. The little bridge you purchased I have written on the back and also sent two or three (views?) I have of Ipswich. . . . .".

From 1875 until his death in 1883 he sent pictures regularly to the Ipswich Art Club exhibitions. They were nearly all of local picturesque views around Ipswich and along the river banks of the Orwell and Gipping. Occasionally he went further afield into Suffolk, to Monks Eleigh, Wickham Market, Marlesford, Dedham and Shotley. He painted watercolours as well as oils. Burrows died at his home at 9 Park Place, Norwich Road, Ipswich and was buried at the Ipswich Cemetery.

Bibliography:

Day, H. & A. E. *East Anglian Painters* Vol. I (Eastbourne, 1967)

References:

Traditional account of R. Burrows, by friend of J. L. Burrows 1974 (Ipswich Museums).

Letter to William Davy (Suffolk Record Office q A759).

Snell, S., Biographical notes on R. Burrows (Suffolk Record Office).

SAMUEL READ (1815-1883)

16a The Grand Chapel and High Altar, Toledo 1876

Watercolour and gouache 66.7 x 52.2cm.
Signed and dated, bottom left: *S. Read*   (R1919-14)
1876

16b The South Porch of the Cathedral Münster 1882

Watercolour and gouache 31.9 x 23.7cm.
Signed and dated, bottom left: *S. Read*   (R1919-15)
1882

These pictures appeared at the exhibitions of the Society of Painters in Watercolours, Pall Mall in 1876 and 1882 respectively. They were acquired by Major V. P. Misa whose collection was sold at Christies 15th May 1919. They were purchased from this sale by Ipswich Museums.

Samuel Read was born at Needham Market in Suffolk, the son of Thomas Read, a shoemaker, and was educated at the town's Grammar School. Around 1830, Read became a clerk to the attorney John Eddowes Sparrowe at the house in the Buttermarket (now known as the Ancient House), Ipswich. Sparrowe was the Town Clerk and backbone of the local Tory party and from 1835 to 1838 Read produced political cartoons supporting the "Blues". Read knew Charles Keene (1823-1891), Sparrowe's nephew, whose portait he sketched in 1832. Read was a member of the Ipswich Society of Professional and Amateur Artists founded in 1832, (see Introduction p.vi), and knew (outside the Society), **Edward Robert Smythe,** Walter Hagreen and Fred Brett Russel.

Between 1837 and 1838 Read drew a set of eighty caricature portraits of Ipswich people and from 1838 to 1842 contributed illustrations to several Ipswich publications.

Later Read worked for the town surveyor William Mason, but in 1841 he joined the Whymper brothers (wood-engravers, originally from Ipswich) as a draughtsman. Read worked for the *Illustrated London News* from 1844 and became the manager of the art department. He travelled throughout Britain and the Continent as a roving reporter and recorded the Crimean War. He specialised in picturesque secular and religious buildings and published *Leaves from a Sketchbook* in 1875.

His watercolours were shown at the Royal Academy, the Society of British Artists, the Society of Painters in Watercolours and the Ipswich Art Club exhibitions (from 1875). Read collected watercolours by Samuel Prout (1783-1852), J. F. Lewis (1805-1876) and David Roberts (1796-1864), all European travellers and popular exponents of picturesque architectural 'topography'. Roberts had produced *The Interior of the Church of San Miguel, Xeres* 1834 (British Museum) after his tour of Spain in 1832. Read often visited Spain and sent Toledo subjects to the exhibitions from at least 1866. The watercolours illustrated here vividly display the atmospheric splendour of European cathedrals in a myriad of luminous details.

Bibliography:
Blatchly, J., *Eighty Ipswich Portraits: Samuel Read's Early Victorian Sketchbook* (Ipswich, 1980).
Scarfe, N., *Views a Painter might Crave: Samuel Read, Charles Keene and Late-Georgian Ipswich Suffolk* COUNTRY LIFE, 5.11.1981 .
References:
SC: 12.5.1883 Obituary; IJ: 12.5.1883 Obituary; ILN: 10.5.1883 Obituary; Catalogue of Read's sale of effects 29.2.1884 (Suffolk Record Office).

JOHN DUVALL (1816-1892)

17   **The Suffolk Show in Christchurch Park** 1869

Oil on canvas 82.3 x 153cm.

Signed, bottom right: *J Duvall.*

(R1939-98)

This was commissioned by Colonel Frederick Barlow who maintained a Racing Stable and stud at "The Shrubbery", Hasketon, Suffolk. It passed to his descendents who presented it to the Ipswich Museums as a gift in 1939.

This painting shows Colonel Barlow in the centre, with his prize-winning Suffolk Punch *Dalesman*, at the Suffolk Show in Christchurch Park (which was at that time private property owned by Thomas Neale Fonnereau). Beside him is his son Eustace and behind him (on horseback in profile) is Chapman his groom riding *Topstall.* On the far right is a group of four men who are (from right to left): Isaac Smith, Bailiff and stallion man to Col. Barlow, holding prize-winner *King of the Dale,* Nat Barthrop of Cretingham, Boby of Stutton, Ipswich and Nat Symonds of Thistleton Hall, Burgh. Standing behind *Dalesman's* rear (in profile and wearing a top hat) is Thomas Brown Esq. of Old Lodge, Uckfield, Sussex and behind him (on the left in a fawn coloured suit facing the viewer) is Richard Garret. On the far left of the picture under the tree is (from left to right): the artist's son and Robert Bond. Ransome can be seen in his four-wheeled pony chais in the middle distance. The gentleman lying on the ground smoking a pipe on the right foreground is John Duvall himself, with a sketch of a man and horse.

John Duvall was born in Kent from a family of Hugenot descent. He came to Ipswich from Ramsgate as a portrait painter. The popularity of photography prompted him to specialise in painting horses. In White's 1855 Directory he appears as "artist and teacher of drawing" at Westgate Street, his home being in Anglesea Road at this time. After 1879 he moved his studio to 4, Buttermarket and from 1881 he was living at 5, Handford Villas, Ranelagh Road. In 1868 he exhibited at the Fine Arts and Industrial Exhibition at The New Assembly Room, Northgate Street. He sent work to the Royal Academy exhibitions from 1855 to 1877.

The idea for the formation of the Ipswich Fine Art Club came out of conversation between Sir Edward Packard (1843-1932) and John Duvall while they were out sketching by the river in 1873. Packard became the Club's first Secretary in 1874 and Duvall a committee member. Duvall exhibited with the Club until 1889.

Duvall was employed by Herman Biddell, a farmer at Playford and first secretary of the Suffolk Horse Society (founded in 1877) to illustrate Volume I of the *Suffolk Stud Book* published in 1880. Several horse owners commissioned oil portraits of Suffolk Punches from Duvall and many of these are now in the Suffolk Horse Society Collection. He also received commissions from the Royal Family e.g. H.R.H. The Princess of Wales, and titled families such as the Duke of Hamilton and the Duke of Westminster. As well as Suffolk, he painted in Kent, Dorset, Wales, Jersey, Scotland and Devon.

Bibliography:

Ryder-Davies, P., *The Suffolk Punch: The County Breed of Cart Horse* (Exh. Cat. Ipswich Museums, 1980)

Parry, A., Webber, M., *Centenary Exhibition of the Ipswich Art Club 1874-1974* (Ipswich, 1975)

References:

East Anglian Miscellany, 1947 p. 14 No. 11586 — *John Duvall of Ipswich* (Suffolk Record Office)

Ipswich Cemetery Records

Notes of H. C. Lewcock 1961 (Ipswich Museums)

JOHN MOORE (1821-1902)

18 **'Fishing Smacks off the East Coast'**

Oil on panel 30.3 x 45.7cm.

Signed, bottom left: *J Moore*

(R1931-28.8)

This was collected by Robert Allen of Ipswich (1848-1920), and bequeathed by his widow Mrs Rosalie Allen to the Ipswich Museums in 1931.

John Moore was born at Woodbridge the son of Martin Moore, a mariner, and Elizabeth Warren, who had married at St Mary's Church in the town in 1815. His date of birth is confirmed by his baptism at the church in 1821 and the words on his tombstone at Ipswich cemetery which say that he died in 1902 "Aged 81 years".

Little is known about his early life in Woodbridge. He married Caroline (c1822-1877) and had a son John Gordon in 1843. In the records of baptism for his son at St. Mary's, John Moore is described as a Brazier by trade and his address is Theatre Street. Early traditional accounts of his life say that he was apprenticed to a "tinker and coppersmith". This is more likely to have been something to do with the work of a "Martin Moore, (engraver)" of the Thorofare in Woodbridge, who was listed in White's 1855 Directory under "Braziers and Tinners", and in the 1841 census return as "Brook Street, Martin Moore, 35 (Age), Brazier, Not born in Suffolk'. John Moore could have met **Thomas Churchyard** and **George James Rowe** in Woodbridge, who admired the work of Constable and Crome. According to the traditional account, Moore moved to Ipswich at around the age of thirty to thirty-five (about 1851 to 1856) where he worked for Jacob Lucas of Orwell Place on decorative work such as wood-graining and sign-writing. He lived at Charles Street and later at George Street and Tower Ramparts. His wife died in 1877 but he re-married in 1878 Harriet Kersey (1838-1900) at St Mary's Church, Woodbridge.

From 1875 to 1901 he was an active exhibitor with the Ipswich Art Club and in 1880 he showed a record of seventeen paintings there. He specialised as a marine artist but produced several landscapes and topographical views of Ipswich.

The real title of the picture illustrated here cannot be discovered from the Art Club lists. The trawling operations of the Suffolk or Essex fisherman in their boats are accurately painted. However, Moore often repeated pictorial formulae and was a "very quick worker", satisfying his mainly local middle-class patrons with pictures for their drawing-room walls. The low-lying terrain in this picture probably indicates that it is the Suffolk or Essex coastline, although it was not beyond Moore to invent scenes from his imagination.

References:

Parish Registers St. Mary's Church, Woodbridge
Ipswich Cemetery Records
Whites Suffolk Directory 1855
Census Returns for Woodbridge 1841
Notes by Alfred East of Ipswich June 1929 (Ipswich Museums).

JOHN MOORE (1821-1902)

19 Northumberland Coast Scene c1877-early 1880's

Oil on canvas 40 x 57.3cm.

Signed, bottom left: *J. Moore.*

(R1938-135)

This was presented to Ipswich Museums by Col. John Josselyn C.M.G., D.S.O., O.B.E., T.D., in 1938.

Traditional accounts say that in 1877 Moore went to Scotland to execute a commission for the Cobbold family. A number of Northumberland seascapes by Moore appeared at the Ipswich Art Club exhibitions in 1877, 1878, 1880 and 1882 which indicate that he toured the area at the same time. He painted large canvases of Holy Island (Ipswich Museums), the Castle and Lindisfarne Abbey and Dustanburgh Castle. In 1889 he was painting Scottish scenes of the Clyde, Ayrshire and the Kyles of Bute.

It is likely that Moore would have been aware of seascapes by the Sunderland marine artist Clarkson Stanfield (1793-1867), named after the Ipswich anti-slavery lobbyist Thomas Clarkson. Stanfield was probably remembered in Suffolk for his sketches in John Murray's eight-volume edition of poetry by Aldeburgh's George Crabbe (1754-1832) and his visits to the area to prepare them in 1833. One painting produced by Stanfield at this time was *Orford on the Ore* (Wallace Collection, London). In addition Stanfield's dramatic scenes of shipwrecks and fishermen at sea were popularised through printed reproductions and he regularly exhibited at the London exhibitions. Another possible influence on Moore's work were the seascapes of Joseph Stannard (1797-1830) and his brother Alfred Stannard (1827-1885) of Norwich, which were finding their way into East Anglian art collections and salerooms.

During his lifetime, Moore's marine paintings were "greatly prized". In 1902, the writer of his obituary noted: "In the rendering of boisterous seas and breakers he had no local superior, whilst he could hold his own in landscape painting, ... Thatched cottages, village commons, rural homesteads, winding rivers, wayside ponds etc., had for him a special attraction, and he always had an eye for the pictureque in whatever he submitted to canvas, whilst in his quiet and unassuming style was reflected the personal character of the artist".

Moore painted marine views of the Ipswich Docks, the shores of the Orwell, Felixstowe, Bawdsey, Aldeburgh, Walberswick, Southwold and Lowestoft as well as the Norfolk broads, Cromer, Yarmouth and Walton-on-the-Naze.

He died at Diss having "wielded the brush with unabated vigour till almost the very last".

Bibliography:
Day, H. A. E., *East Anglian Painters* Vol. I (Eastbourne, 1967)
Tyne & Wear County Council Museums, *Clarkson Stanfield* (Exh. Cat., 1979)
References:
IJ: 12.4.1902 Obituary

THOMAS SMYTHE (1825-1906)

20 **'Interior with Dogs'**

Oil on canvas 35.3 x 53cm.
Signed, bottom left: *T. Smythe*
(R1965-1)

This was passed to Ipswich Museums from Ipswich Town Hall where it had been kept for many years. Its previous source is unknown.

Thomas Smythe was fifteen years younger than his brother **Edward Smythe.** It is probable that he also lived in Berner's Street, Ipswich and attended Robert Burcham Clamp's school (which had closed by 1836) for a short time.

After working with Edward from around 1846 to 1850 (by which time Edward had left for Bury St. Edmunds), Thomas set up independently as a landscape and animal painter at Brook Street, Ipswich. In 1855 he married a Miss Pearse of Ipswich and had three sons and two daughters. Thomas, the eldest son, was also an artist but died tragically in a cycling acident at the age of nineteen in 1881. Ernest, his second son, worked in London as a book illustrator and became an examiner at the Royal Drawing Society. One of Thomas Smythe's daughters married Frank Brown, an Ipswich architect and biographer of **George Frost** in 1895 (see Plate 3).

Thomas Smythe exhibited paintings at the Royal Academy, the Society of British Artists, and at Manchester. Like his brother, he was a staunch supporter of the Ipswich Art Club from its opening exhibition in 1875 to 1899. Both Thomas and Edward Smythe took part in the Fine Art and Industrial Exhibition held at the New Assembly Rooms in Northgate Street, in connection with The Working Mens College, in 1868. Most of Thomas Smythe's work was sold locally, whereas Edward's reputation was more widespread. Thomas's pictures were also smaller in scale and his subject matter was probably even more sentimental and idealised than Edward's.

One of his specialities was the winter landscape, showing inn and coaching scenes, skating, boys snowballing, wood gatherers or people trudging to market with their horse and cart. He did many "cottage door" subjects in the manner of Morland and rustic genre scenes of cottage interiors or itinerant musicians and performers surrounded by a village audience. Smythe actually found the Old Plough Inn, Kensall Green in London which George Morland had frequently visited. He painted it, with the fact of its association included in the title, when it was shown at the Ipswich Art Club exhibition in 1898. He often included animals, especially horses and dogs, wherever possible in his scenes and would have absorbed the same appreciation as his brother of the popular animal painting of Edwin Landseer.

This painting of four dogs by a hearth could be either *Their Fireside,* shown in the Ipswich Art Club exhibition of 1894 or *Their own Fireside* shown there in 1896. The artist has delighted in the details of ordinary objects within the cottage interior, from the humble meal at the table (painted simply within the Dutch still life tradition), to the hat on the chair and the vegetables by the wooden pail on the floor.

Bibliography:
See Plates 12 & 13

References:
EADT: 17.5. 1906 Obituary

THOMAS SMYTHE (1825-1906)

21 Fishing Boats at Southwold

Watercolour, gouache & pencil 19 x 33.5cm.

Signed, bottom right: *T. Smythe*

(R1916-6)

This was bequeathed to Ipswich Museums by T. Edward Jones in 1916.

Few watercolours by Thomas Smythe are known, although it appears he was certainly master of the medium. He frequently visited Southwold to paint, and sent views of the Suffolk coastal town to the 1879, 1882 and 1889 Ipswich Art Club exhibitions.

There is a fresh out-of-doors quality about this seascape (one of a pair), in which Thomas Smythe effectively conveys light and atmosphere. It is a sharp contrast to the unchanging, enclosed and comfortably predictable world of his oil-painted rustic scenes of peasant life. Here the wind from the sea billows out the sails of the fishing boat and the sunlight reflects off the sand and sea-foam. Subtle lines and delicate colouring, with Smythe's occasional characteristic touches of red, make this picture a refreshing surprise for all followers of his work.

Thomas Smythe lived in Ipswich until the death of his brother Edward in 1899. After then he lived with his son Ernest in London until the end of his life.

Bibliography:
See Plate 20

HENRY GEORGE TODD (1847-1898)

22   Gainsborough Lane, Ipswich 1888

Oil on canvas 30.8 x 40.8cm.

Signed, bottom right: *H G. Todd*
                      1888

(R1931-28.52)

This picture, and its pair, were collected by Robert Allen of Ipswich (1848-1920), and bequeathed by his widow Mrs Rosalie Allen to Ipswich Museums in 1931.

Henry George Todd was born at Bury St. Edmunds, the eldest son of George Todd, a talented docorative artist, who ran a substantial painting and decorating business from St. Andrew's Street North. After studying at the County School, Bury, young Henry Todd obtained a place at the Kensington Schools of Art (now the Royal College of Art) around 1864. After studying there for three years, he returned to Bury St. Edmunds to assist his father with specialist decorative work such as woodgraining, gilding and signwriting.

Todd moved to Ipswich to work for Thomas Stearn & Sons of Fore Street and Key Street, as a gilder and signwriter. At about this time, he married Lucy Ellen Quinton and lived at Waterloo Road. They had two sons and three daughters. Todd left Stearn's to become a full time artist. According to the family account, he took on a house and studio in Unitarian Gardens (also known as Priory Place) where, between 1887 and 1892, he produced some of his finest paintings. Included amongst these was his *Still Life* of 1888, his only exhibit at the Royal Academy. During his lifetime, Todd also exhibited at the Dudley Gallery and the Society of British Artists.

Although he was chiefly a painter of still life, he also produced landscapes. The family account says that he "was a lover of the countryside and frequently fished the Gipping. He painted a good number of landscapes of the environs of Ipswich, his oak trees were beautifully painted with fine detail".

Gainsborough Lane, leading down to the shores of the River Orwell, had become a popular haunt for artists since the eighteenth century, when **Thomas Gainsborough** had sketched there (see Introduction p.iv). The pair to Todd's version of the famous Lane, seen here, shows a vista through the trees to the river, with children playing on the side of the track. Todd also exhibited two views of *Gainsborough's Lane* at the Ipswich Art Club exhibition in 1887.

References:
Notes of Mr. J. V. Todd 1974/5.

HENRY GEORGE TODD (1847-1898)

23a **'Still Life, with Ewer'** 1892

Oil on canvas 51 x 41cm.

Signed, bottom right: *H. G. Todd.*
1892.

(R1931-28.51)

This was collected by Robert Allen of Ipswich (1848-1920), and bequeathed by his widow Mrs Rosalie Allen to Ipswich Museums in 1931.

23b **'Still Life, with Delft Vase'** c1890's

Oil on canvas 61.2 x 51cm.

Monogram, bottom right.

(R1961-170)

The source of this picture is unknown.

Henry George Todd became a specialist in the painting of fruit. Most of the still life paintings he exhibited at the Ipswich Art Club from 1875 to 1897 were called simply *Fruit* or *Still Life*. Therefore it is not possible to identify the titles of the paintings illustrated here from the Art Club lists. *'Still Life, with Delft Vase'* was wrongly attributed to E. Ladell until the Todd family found a vase in their possession identical to the one in the picture and recognised it as Henry Todd's work. The monogram in the bottom right corner (possibly not original to the painting) had misled everyone until this discovery. The Todd family also owns the ewer which appears in Plate a.

According to the family account, Todd had "access to the finest hot-house grapes which he himself cut from the vine, taking care not to erase the bloom".

Todd's compositions were based on the seventeenth century Dutch still life tradition of artists such as Willem Kalf and Abraham van Beyeren, who produced pictures known as "Table" or "Breakfast" pieces. Their opulent arrangements of heaps of objects, painted in meticulous detail, were intended as decorative fantasies in tribute to household hospitality. Such paintings were popular with Victorian collectors and Todd, with the Ladells of Colchester, found a receptive market for this type of picture.

Bibliography:
Robertson, A., & Strickland-Constable, M., *The Irresistible Object: Still Life 1600-1985* (Exh. Cat. Leeds City Art Galleries, 1985)
References:
Notes of J. V. Todd 1974/5
EADT: 21.2.1967 & Ipswich Evening Star: 20.2.1967. J. Todd and the family vase.

HENRY ROBERTSON (1848-1930)

24 **Blythburgh** 1887

Watercolour 30.6 x 50.3cm.

Monogram, bottom right.

(R1968-79)

This appeared in the Ipswich Art Club exhibition of 1887 but was not sold. It was presented to Ipswich Museums in 1968 by Miss Pauline Robertson.

This scene was taken from a bend in the River Blyth, looking eastwards across the marsh to Blythburgh Church.

Henry Robertson was possibly born in Liverpool but little is known about his early life. Around 1859 he attended Mansion Grammar School, Leatherhead, and married Hamilton Barclay in 1877. His cousin Charles Robertson (1844-1897) and his cousin's son Percy Robertson (1868/9-1934), were both eminent artists.

From 1880 to 1894 Henry Robertson lived in Ipswich. From 1881 to 1885 he was at Burlington Road and from 1888 he lived at 102 Christchurch Street. He sent nearly three hundred works to the Ipswich Art Club exhibitions from 1883 to 1898. (His cousin Percy also sent work to the Club from 1886 to 1905). The Robertsons moved to Tonbridge in Kent from 1894 to 1898, went on to Norwich and finally settled in Bromley, where Robertson died at the age of eighty-two.

A small private income enabled Robertson to pursue an artist's career despite his weak eyesight. In 1886 he became an Associate Member of the Royal Society of Painter-Etchers and Engravers and exhibited at the Royal Academy in 1888, 1892 and 1894. Robertson produced mainly marine subjects in watercolours and etchings and enjoyed the busy shipyards, docks and riverside scenes of Ipswich by night and day. He also painted the East Coast at Aldeburgh, Harwich, Lowestoft and Southwold. This view of *Blythburgh* in Suffolk would have been produced during the period when **Philip Wilson Steer** was working at nearby Walberswick.

Robertson built up his topographical watercoloured views from a brush and sepia drawing overlaid with transparent colour washes and finished with small dashes of paint to bring out the details. His accuracy was assisted by the use of family photographs. In this painting, he has unified the landscape by showing the windswept marshes, caught by the same breeze that ripples over the flowing River Blyth and chases the broken clouds across the expansive Suffolk sky.

Bibliography:
Henry Robertson A.R.E. 1848-1930 (Exh. Cat. Reading Museum & Art Gallery, 1987)

References:
Notes on the Robertson Family by John Griffin (Ipswich Museums)

FREDERIC GEORGE COTMAN (1850-1920)

25   The Dame School 1887

Oil on canvas 36 x 50.2cm.

Signed and dated, bottom right: *F. G. Cotman 1887*

(R 1961-77)

This was shown at the Ipswich Art Club exhibition of 1887 where Peter Bruff bought it. He bequeathed it (with Plate 13) to Ipswich Borough Council in 1900, and it later passed to the Museums.

Frederic George Cotman was born at 186 Wycks Bishop Street, St Clements, Ipswich the youngest son of Maria Taylor and Henry Edmund Cotman, a silk mercer of Norwich (whose older brother was John Sell Cotman (1782-1842)).

Between 1866 and 1867 Cotman was a private pupil of William Thompson Griffiths, the headmaster of the Ipswich School of Art, and he assisted Griffiths with classes at the School as well as teaching at smaller local schools. His work was exhibited for the first time in 1867 at the Eastern Counties Working Classes Industrial Exhibition Norwich, where he won a prize medal. In 1868 he became a student at the Royal Academy Schools where, a couple of years later, **Walter Batley** followed him from the Ipswich School of Art. Cotman's proficiency as a draughtsman and painter in oils and watercolour was rewarded by four silver medals and a gold, which he won at the RA. His gold medal work for the best historical painting, *The Death of Eucles* 1873, was bought by public subscription for the town of Ipswich (but it was later misguidedly sold). A fellow student at this time was **William Symonds.**

His teachers, Frederick Leighton (1830-1896) and Henry Tanworth Wells (1828-1903), both employed him on their own paintings. During the holidays he assisted the still-life painter Edward Ladell of Colchester. Cotman rapidly became established as a London society portrait painter and also produced homely genre scenes such as *One of the Family* 1880 (Walker Art Gallery, Liverpool) which is perhaps his most famous picture.

The Dame School followed earlier examples of this type of genre painting, such as William Bromley's (fl.1835-1888) *The Schoolroom* 1861 (location unknown) and *The Captured Truant,* 1854 by Thomas Brooks (1818-1891). Thomas Faed (1826-1900) produced *The School Board in the Cottage* (Private Collection) as late as 1892, indicating that the Victorian taste for this type of subject had not diminished.

Bibliography:
Baldry, A. L., *An East Anglian Painter: Frederic George Cotman R.I.* THE STUDIO, Vol 47, No 197, 14th August 1909
Watt, N., *Frederic George Cotman RI ROI 1850-1920: Pictures from the Cotman Family Collection* (Exh. cat. Norwich Museums 1983)
Wood, C., *Victorian Panorama: Paintings of Victorian Life* (London, 1976)
See Plate 26
References:
EADT: 13.12.1873 Ipswich Students at the Royal Academy

FREDERIC GEORGE COTMAN (1850-1920)

26   Farmyard and Dovecotes, Nettlestead 1912

Oil on board 23.3 x 38.8cm.

Signed and dated, bottom right: *F. G. Cotman 1912.*

(R1958-36)

This was bequeathed to the Ipswich Museums by Mrs. F. E. Parkington in 1958.

In 1882 Cotman was elected a member of the Royal Institute of Painters in Water Colour and in 1883, a member of the Royal Institute of Oil Painters. He sent exhibits to them both until 1916.

In 1875 he married Ann Barclay Grahame of Morphie, Scotland and also in that year became a founder member of the Ipswich Art Club, to which he sent regular contributions. He was a member until his death in 1920, and was elected its President in 1899.

He acquired a studio at Hemingford Grey, Huntingdonshire around 1901 to 1902, after a long period in London, and in 1905 moved to Ives. By 1916 he was living at Harland House, Felixstowe and died at 49 Quilter Road there. He was buried at Old Felixstowe Church.

Cotman painted many East Anglian landscapes and towards the end of his life his work gradually became more impressionistic. In 1905 he exhibited in Norwich with **Alfred Munnings,** whose approach to landscape was sympathetic to his own. The Ipswich Museums & Galleries collection has several landscapes by Cotman showing misty sun-filled scenes around the rural environs of Ipswich and the River Orwell. After seeing pictures in the National Gallery by Turner he recorded in his diary, as early as 1867: "They brought to my remembrance scenes and subjects of mist I myself observed in nature, much fancy and imagination combined with nature which enheightens their value . . . which ought most certainly be caught at and depicted".

Bibliography:
Watt, N., *F. G. Cotman — A Man of More Than Ordinary Strength of Personality* NORFOLK FAIR, May 1984
See Plate 25.

WALTER D. BATLEY (1850-1936)

27 Minsmere Cliff, Dunwich 1897

Oil on canvas 60.8 x 122.5cm.

Signed and dated, bottom left: *Walter D. Batley 1897*

(R1897-12)

This was purchased from the Ipswich Art Club exhibition of 1897 by Felix Thornley Cobbold, who presented it to Ipswich Museums.

Walter Daniel Batley was born in Westgate Street, Ipswich, one of five children of Henry Baring Batley, who owned a house decorating business, and his wife Maria. Walter's delicate health led to the purchase of a seaside cottage at Felixstowe in 1860 where Walter lived with his mother after she became a widow. Often too ill to go out, he spent his time drawing and painting.

He studied at the Ipswich School of Art under W. T. Griffiths. Only a couple of years before, **Frederic George Cotman** had been a leading student and assistant at the School before going on to the Royal Academy Schools. Walter followed a similar course, later moving to London to live with his brother Henry and probably meeting up with Cotman as a fellow student at the R.A. During this period, Walter was chosen to copy the Raphael Cartoons for the Government, and in 1874 he won the South Kensington's Gold Medal for figure drawing. It is possible that he may have met Stanhope A. Forbes (1857-1947) at around this time, whose later work he greatly admired.

In 1875 he exhibited for the first time at the Royal Academy, a landscape entitled, in the fashion of the day, *How calm, how beautiful comes on, the stilly hours when storms are gone*. He sent work there until 1901 and also to the Society of British Artists.

In the same year, he was a founder member of the Ipswich Art Club, with Cotman, and served on its committee for several years. He was made an Honorary member in 1935. He continued to regularly exhibit with the Club until his death. Although Batley experimented with narrative genre in the 1880's he was primarily a landscape painter.

In 1889 the Batley family was living at 'Little Roundwood' on the corner of Sidegate Lane at Rushmere, where the trees and cottages became his favourite subjects. Between 1880 and 1910 he went on painting trips to Cornwall, Yorkshire and Derbyshire. Dunwich, Aldeburgh, Walberswick and Southwold were amongst Batley's Suffolk subjects. It is possible that he could have met **Philip Wilson Steer,** who was painting at Walberswick during the 1880's, since by the turn of the century Batley was showing an interest in new kinds of atmospheric landscape imagery and his paint was applied with greater freedom and energy. In paintings such as *Minsmere Cliff, Dunwich* he reduced the landscape to its bare essentials, and captured the effects of reflected sunlight on the Dunwich shoreline.

After living a short time at Felixstowe, the Batleys finally settled at 'The Anchorage' Cauldwell Hall Road Ipswich in 1928.

Bibliography:
Bennett, C., MacDonald, M., *Walter Batley 1850-1936, An Artist for all Seasons* (Exh. cat. Ipswich Museums, 1988)
References:
EADT: 4.1.1890 *A Visit to the Studios* (of W. Batley and E. Lingwood)

WILLIAM R. SYMONDS (1851-1934)

28 Girl with a Silver Fish

Oil on canvas 73.6 x 48.4cm.

Signed, bottom right: *W. R. Symonds*
1889

(R1911-9)

This was shown at the Ipswich Art Club exhibition of 1911, where it was purchased by Ipswich Museums.

William Robert Symonds was born at Yoxford, Suffolk, the son of Nathaniel Symonds, a grocer and draper, and Susannah Cotton. He studied at the Ipswich School of Art under W. T. Griffiths, where his contemporaries were **Walter D. Batley** and **Frederic George Cotman.** Symonds went on to the Royal Academy Schools where, in 1873, he was awarded the "premium for the best drawing from the Antique". Cotman was a fellow student at this time. He spent several months studying at Antwerp and on his return he specialised in portrait painting.

His most famous portrait is of *Sir Richard Wallace* 1885, in the Wallace Collection, London. It was presented to Sir Richard and Lady Wallace by the Tenants and Friends of the Sudbourne Estate in Suffolk. Wallace was the High Steward of the Borough of Ipswich. It was the only picture by a living British artist to be represented in the Wallace Collection, which opened to the public in 1900, following Lady Wallace's bequest to the Nation.

Another celebrated painting was *At the Market Gate* 1880 (location unknown) which contrasted a haggard old lady and a sweet young girl selling flowers.

Until 1880, Symonds lived in Ipswich at 21 Fore Street and Soane Street where he had a studio in one of the Park lodges (since demolished). From 1881 he was at Holland Park Road London and from 1893, Cornwall Lodge, Rowan Road Brook Green.

Symonds painted many portraits of children of well-to-do families and also fantasy pieces such as *The Princess and the Frog* 1894 (Bradford City Art Gallery & Museums). His range is well illustrated in an article in the *Windsor Magazine* of 1910.

As well as at the Royal Academy, Symonds exhibited work at the Grosvenor Gallery, New Gallery and elsewhere in London. He undertook several mayoral portraits in Ipswich which are now in the Ipswich Museums' collection. His work is also represented at the Army Medical School, Queen's College Belfast, the Royal Victorian Hospital Netley, and Oriel College, Magdalen College and Pembroke College Oxford.

Symonds was a regular exhibitor at the Ipswich Art club exhibitions from 1875 until his death. He was elected President of the Club in 1889.

Bibliography:
Chester, A., *The Art of Mr. W. R. Symonds* WINDSOR MAGAZINE, April 1910, pp577-592.
References:
Ipswich Observer & Felixstowe Times: 20.7.1907 *Ipswich Man of Note. Mr W. R. Symonds* p.6; IJ: 13.12.1873 Ipswich Students at RA; Thieme-Becker, *Künstler-Lexikon* Vol XXXII (Leipzig, 1927) p.362; Census Returns for 1851.

THE HON. DUFF TOLLEMACHE (1859-1936)

29 **After the Catch** c1885

Oil on canvas 60.8 x 45.5cm.
Signed, bottom left: *Duff Tollemache* (R1928-10)

Duff Tollemache exhibited this painting at the Ipswich Art Club exhibition in 1885. It was purchased by Sterling Westhorpe, and later acquired by William Eade. Ipswich Museums purchased it from the sale of Eade's pictures in January 1928.

Duff Tollemache was the seventh son of John, 1st Lord Tollemache of Helmingham, and grandson of Admiral John Richard Delap Tollemache, from whom he may have inherited a love of the sea. His unusual christian name came from the maiden name of his mother, Eliza Georgina Duff.

Until 1953, Helmingham Hall contained a good collection of British eighteenth century landscape paintings by artists such as Richard Wilson, George Morland and **Thomas Gainsborough** (see Plate 1). Tollemache would have remembered the five full length portraits by Sir Joshua Reynolds which were sold in 1888. The Tollemaches also owned estates in Northamptonshire and Cheshire. In 1888 they bought the Ipswich Brewery and successfully operated it as Tollemache Breweries Ltd. It was probably appropriate that Duff Tollemache should marry a girl named Emily Beer in 1897!

Duff Tollemache studied art at the Royal Academy Schools and the Academie Julian in Paris. He found work in the studios of the sea painter Francois Musin in Brussels, and Leon Bonnat and Alfred Stevens in Paris. He painted several portraits, and examples of these can be seen at Helmingham Hall eg *John, 1st Baron Tollemache of Helmingham* (1889). However, his real love of seascape was demonstrated by the subjects he sent to the Royal Academy exhibitions from 1899 to 1932. Many scenes were of Cornwall and the Scilly Isles. Tollemache does not appear to have visited Newlyn on the Cornish coast, which by 1900 was fading as an artistic centre. However his heavy "square brush technique" used in *After the Catch* (probably a Cornish scene), may have been learned from the Newlyn painters, who were criticised for using this type of painterly touch. Tollemache also adopted their treatment of light and atmosphere which blurred the definition of objects. A similar painterly technique was used in *Portsmouth Harbour,* a large oil completed in 1885 (Helmingham Hall), in which the *HMS Victory* is pulled in by tugs under an oppressive grey sky. Tollemache's work was shown at the Paris Salon and a number of international exhibitions. He knew Frederick Roe (1864-1947), an artist with family connections at Ashbocking in Suffolk, who was an exhibitor at the Ipswich Art Club from 1890 to 1891. Tollemache gave Roe a watercolour called *Off the Scilly Isles* which had been exhibited at the Royal Institute of Painters in Water Colour in 1925. From 1888, he was based in London, changing his address several times until 1899, when he appears to have settled at 131 Oakwood Court, Kensington. Nevertheless, throughout his life Tollemache maintained contact with his family at Helmingham and, as a member of the Ipswich Art Club from 1881 to 1931, regularly sent paintings to the annual exhibitions. He is known to have produced one Suffolk coastal scene called *Lowestoft Trawlers* (unknown location).

Bibliography:
Roe, F.G., *Sea Painters of Britain from Constable to Brangwyn* (Leigh-on-Sea, 1948)
Waterhouse, E., *The Collection of Pictures in Helmingham Hall* (Suffolk, 1958)
Who's Who in Art, 2nd & 3rd editions, 1929 & 1934.

PHILIP WILSON STEER (1860-1942)

30 **Knucklebones, Walberswick** 1888-1889

Oil on canvas 61 x 76.2cm.

Signed, bottom left: *P. W. Steer*

(R1947-31.23)

This painting was exhibited at the London Impressionists exhibition held at the Grupil Gallery in 1889. It was owned by Geoffrey Blackwell and later acquired by Herbert E. West, who presented it to Ipswich Museums in 1947.

Philip Wilson Steer was born at Birkenhead and was descended from a line of Devonshire farmers and shipbuilders. He probably received his early art education from his father Philip Steer (1810-1871), who painted landscapes and portraits. He enjoyed the hobby of collecting minerals and fossils as well as painting when he was young, and had an opportunity to join the Department of Coins and Medals at the British Museum. The examinations for the Civil Service were too academically demanding for him and so he decided to become a painter.

He went to the Gloucester College of Art between 1878 and 1880, studying under John Kemp, before going on to the South Kensington Schools in London in 1880 and 1881. Failing to get into the Royal Academy Schools, Steer went to the Academie Julian, a renowned "alternative" art school, in Paris. He later transferred to the Ecole des Beaux Arts as a pupil of Alexandra Cabanel (1823-1889) a painter of classical subjects who maintained the academic system of copying from the Antique. At this time Steer could have seen some of the new developments in French painting in the Paris Salons of 1882 and 1883. He also could have visited the private galleries in Paris where the works of Monet and other artists were shown.

In 1884 Steer visited the retrospective exhibition of work by Edouard Manet (1832-1883) at the Ecole des Beaux Arts and during that summer, he returned to England, having failed to pass the French language and history examination at the Ecole. He went on to Walberswick where he painted for the rest of the warm months. He adopted an Impressionist technique of flecked brushstrokes in bright colours.

Every summer from 1884 Steer painted landscapes and seascapes away from his London studio in Chelsea and regularly stayed at Walberswick. By 1887 to 1888, Steer had become the leading "English Impressionist". With a number of like-minded artists, he founded the New English Art Club in 1886 which allied itself to the new French painting and was dissatisfied with the traditional Royal Academy system, (see Introduction   ). Through Steer, Walberswick became a popular resort for many other artists. He painted there until 1889 and made infrequent return visits.

By the end of the nineteenth century, Steer was primarily known as a figure painter. He taught at the Slade School from the 1890s where his approach was practical rather than verbal. His main influence was as a colourist and for his modelling through the manipulation of light.

Bibliography:

Laughton, B., *Philip Wilson Steer* (Oxford, 1971)

Munro, J., *Philip Wilson Steer: Paintings & Watercolours* (Exh. cat. Fitzwilliam Museum Cambridge & Arts Council, 1986)

EDWIN THOMAS JOHNS (1862-1947)

31 Memories 1929

Watercolour and gouache 54.5 x 72.6cm.
Signed, bottom right: *E. Thos. Johns*
1929

(R1944-137)

This was purchased by the Ipswich Museums from an exhibition of the artist's work at Tibbenhams Gallery, Ipswich in 1944.

Edwin Thomas Johns was born in Ipswich, the son of a cabinet maker William Johns of 4 Northgate Street. Johns attended the Ipswich School of Art under W. T. Griffiths before being articled to the architect James Butterworth of 6, Museum Street. He joined the practice of Brightwen Binyon (1846-1905), the architect responsible for the Ipswich Corn Exchange, and later moved on to William Eade's office, where he became a partner in the firm. He practiced on his own for a while from his home at 8 Lower Brook Street and was joined by his nephew Martin Slater (1892-1990) in 1921. Johns retired in 1932. He was instrumental in the formation of the Suffolk Association of Architects, and became its first President.

Johns joined the Ipswich Art Club in 1877 and was an active and prominent committee member until the end of his life. He exhibited at the Royal Academy from 1905 to 1939.

The painstaking draughtsmanship and detail evident in Johns' watercolours, was possibly a result of the disciplined art training he had received under Griffiths, where highly finished drawings of casts, fruit and flowers were the order of the day.

Several of Johns' watercolours painted around 1910 to 1930 looked back nostalgically to the work of the mid-Victorian narrative painters. The fate of the exploited seamstress in her garret had been a popular theme with artists since Thomas Hood's poem *The Song of the Shirt* first appeared in *Punch* in 1843. Part of the poem
"For only one short hour, To feel as I used to feel
Before I knew the woes of want, And the walk that costs a meal"
was the title of Anna Blunden's painting of 1854 which was reproduced in the *Illustrated London News* as part of a memorial to the poet.

In *Memories*, Johns includes a prospect across the Ipswich rooftops, which shows the green dome of the Frasers Furniture store in Princes Street which he designed in 1912. It is thought that the women in Johns paintings were often modelled on his wife and also Georgina Collins (1906-1979), who was in service at the Nursing Home in Brook Street. From the 1930's Johns also painted many topographical views of Ipswich docks and streets and travelled abroad.

Eleanor Gribble (1883-1960) produced a pastel portrait of Edwin Johns in 1941. In 1942, in his eightieth year, a portfolio of watercolours and sketches by his contemporary artists in the Ipswich Art Club was presented to him. These, and the portrait, are in the Ipswich Borough Museums & Galleries Collection.

Bibliography:
Wood, C., *Victorian Panorama: Paintings of Victorian Life* (London, 1976).

References:
Ipswich Art Club, 110th Annual Exhibition Catalogue, 1987; Notes by H. C. Lewcock, 1969 (Ipswich Museums).

ELEANOR M. EVERY (1864-1935)

32 Cornfields at Kersey c1900

Watercolour 42 x 56.7cm.

(R1936-72.1)

This was bequeathed to Ipswich Museums by the artist.

Eleanor Maude Every was the second daughter of Sir Henry Flower Every (1830-1893), 10th Baronet of Eggington Hall, near Derby, and Justice of the Peace for Derbyshire and Staffordshire. The hall, completed by the Wyatt family in 1783, was surrounded by an estate of almost two thousand acres. (It was demolished after 1954).

An early talent for drawing was nurtured by a course of teaching Eleanor Every received from Paul Naftel (1817-1891), a successful drawing master from Guernsey who settled in England in 1870 and became Professor of Drawing at Elizabeth College. He was chiefly a watercolourist and a member of the Old Watercolour Society. According to family tradition, Naftel "predicted that if her zeal continued she would go far". After her course of tuition she enjoyed being out "in those Eggington fields, with the River Dove at hand or various brooks. She was also seen making studies in cornfields and showed wonderful patience in returning day after day to get the effect she wanted — The farmer being asked to delay 'carrying' to give her a little more time — In winter she had to be content with studies of interiors & then her patience was again in demand — she made many sketches of the village church — also interiors of part of the old home — the stair-case the front hall with its 2 full-length Romney portraits & achieved wonderful success each time — Other interiors were in cow-sheds in mid-winter — & red-brick farm-buildings were shown under a mass of snow — in sunshine that gave a cheerful atmosphere —".

Eleanor Every painted watercolours all her life and often exhibited at the Society for the Promotion of Art at the Alpine Club where she received many prizes. In 1889 she sent work to exhibitions from Eggington Hall, but by 1900 she was living at 18 Montagu Street, Portman Square, London. She exhibited one work at the Dudley Gallery, one at the Royal Institute of Painters in Water Colour and one with the Society of Woman Artists.

Eleanor's mother, Mary Holland, had originally come from Saxmundham and so there were plenty of relatives to stay with in Suffolk. In addition, Eleanor's nephew, the 11th Baronet Sir Edward Oswald Every (1886-1959), married Ivy Meller of Rushmere near Ipswich in 1909. There could also have been a friendship between Eleanor and Kate Prentice (1845-1911) born in Stowmarket, who also was taught by Paul Naftel, painted landscapes and lived in London.

Eleanor Every produced a number of watercolours of Suffolk scenes including Higham Watermill, Claydon Pit, Cransford Hall, Hadleigh and Aldeburgh. Although it appears that Eleanor Every had a private income and did not need to earn a living by her paintings, she was a dedicated voluntary social-worker in London. After long hours visiting in poor neighbourhoods all day, she returned home in the evenings to complete paintings begun each morning.

References:
Notes of Alice V. Every, the artist's sister c.1950 (Ipswich Museums)
Notes of Mabel Every, the artist's sister 5.3.1936 (Ipswich Museums)
Burke, J., *Peerage Baronetage & Knightage* 105th ed. (London, 1970) p.966.
Craven, M., *The Ancient Families of Derbyshire No. 2 — The Everys* DERBYSHIRE LIFE & COUNTRYSIDE (Nov. 1980)

HARRY BECKER (1865-1928)

33a **Man Hedging** c1913-1928

Oil on canvas board 37.5 x 45.3cm.

(R1954-126.5)

These pictures were presented to the Ipswich Museums by Mrs. H. Becker of Wangford in 1954.

33b **Two Men Clearing the Banks of a Stream** c1913-1928

Oil on canvas board 45.3 x 37.5cm.

(R1954-126.4)

Harry Becker was born in Colchester, one of four sons of Dr Charles Becker, a German. He studied art at the Royal Academy Schools at Antwerp and finished his training after 1884 in the studio of Carolus Duran in Paris, a fashionable portrait painter. Duran rejected the Impressionists, whose work Becker was beginning to admire, particularly Manet and Degas. However, his colour palette was not yet liberated from the darker tones of his tutor. From 1886 to 1894 Becker lived at the Minories in Colchester, and then moved to London where he had a studio until 1913. During these years he regularly visited Kent and East Anglia, and after trips to Holland, he made lithographs of potato pickers in 1909.

In 1902 Becker married Georgina Waddington, herself an artist, and from 1913 they lived at Wenhaston, Suffolk. After 1926 they moved to Hinton, near Darsham, where he remained until his death.

In the country, Beckers life was isolated and poverty-stricken and there were few opportunities for sales. His contempt for the commercialism of the art world, patronage and recognition meant that the family was dependent on Georgina's salary through teaching art at the local school. He hated to part with his pictures and sometimes tried to buy back ones he had sold. As he could not afford good art materials he used almost anything to draw or paint upon. Small notebooks were filled with jottings of his impressions together with details of weather and times of day.

He followed a routine of going out early in the fields with the agricultural workers to draw and paint small oil sketches on the spot, often working on larger paintings with previously prepared sketches by his side.

From 1915 Becker produced posters for the London Underground, to encourage girls to work on the land during the First World War. Becker's work was obsessive and he produced thousands of drawings in pencil, charcoal, red chalk or pen and ink, some etchings and lithographs and paintings in oil and watercolour.

Everything that Becker did was passionately drawn or painted and was never changed or retouched. He captured the slow, repetitive seasonal cycles of agricultural life in his vision of the farmworkers and their relationship to the land and its produce. His unhesitant applications of thick bright oil paint, wide washes of pure watercolour or deep black strokes of pencil and charcoal immortalised the proud Suffolk labourer in the age before the mechanisation of farming.

Bibliography:
Loftus, S., *Harry Becker 1865-1928* (Exh. Cat., Minories Colchester, 1974)

ROSE MEAD (1867-1946)

34 Cottage Interior 1908

Oil on canvas 101.5 x 126cm.

Signed, bottom right: *Rose Mead*

(R1928-189)

This was shown at the Royal Academy in 1908, as "Humble Life", and at the Ipswich Art Club exhibition of 1928, where it was purchased by Ipswich Museums.

Emma Rose Mead was the youngest daughter of Samuel Mead, a plumber and glazier of Hatter Street, Bury St. Edmunds. From about 1885 to 1890 she studied at the Lincoln School of Art with Emily Beatrice Bland (1864-1951) and Frederick Elwell (1870-1958) and later at the Westminster School in London under Frederick Brown (1851-1941). After this she spent a year in Paris in the studio of Delacluse with fellow artist Julia Beatrice How (1867-1932). One of her early pastel portraits was exhibited at the Paris Salon. She was apparently a contemporary and friend of Agustus John (1878-1961).

Rose Mead lived in London for a time, but returned to 18a Crown Street, Bury St. Edmunds where she nursed her sick mother and painted local subjects in her studio. From there she established a busy local practice specialising in portraits, townscapes, and flower studies in oil and watercolours.

Between 1896 and 1939 Rose Mead exhibited two paintings at the Royal Society of Portrait Painters, two at the Royal Cambrian Academy, three at the Society of Women Artists and six at the Royal Academy.

St. Edmundsbury Museums own thirty examples of her work. A large retrospective exhibition, including ninety-three paintings, was held in the Art Gallery in Bury St. Edmunds in 1955.

Rose Mead painted her "low life" or genre scenes and subjects with fluid painterly tones of brown touched with bright splashes of colour. The apples on the table in *Cottage Interior* comprise a remarkable still life study after the manner of Gustave Courbet's (1819-1877) *Apples and Pomegranate*, 1871 (National Gallery, London). During the last decade of the nineteenth century the Newlyn School of Artists had painted popular interior scenes of ordinary working people, often with windows and fireplaces to offer a source of reflected light e.g. *Forging the Anchor*, 1892 (Ipswich Museums). Rose Mead shared their Paris training and interest in French art, although her intuitive application of paint was freer, more lively and perhaps less calculated.

Her obituary in the local paper of 1946 described her as follows:
"She had — no pretensions to greatness, being a woman of marked individualism, and possessing a temperament which made her completely devoted to her art to the exclusion of every other consideration".

References:
Autobiographical letter by Rose Mead 20.11.1932 and newspaper-cutting of 1946 obituary (Ipswich Museums); Entries in family bible belonging to relatives of Rose Mead; EADT: Supplement 19.4.1988 *Portrait of a Bury St. Edmunds Artist.*

GEORGE RUSHTON (1868-1948)

35 'Oleander'

Watercolour 50.5 x 32.8cm.
Signed, bottom right: *G R. RUSHTON*
(R1987-90.2)

This was purchased from Mrs E. Hendry, the artist's daughter, by Ipswich Museums in 1987.

Oleander is a shrub which grows naturally in Mediterranean countries and can only grow as an indoor plant in Britain. Therefore these cut flowers probably were painted by Rushton while he was abroad.

Born at Birmingham, Rushton began an engineering career, studying at the City Art School in his spare time in order to obtain his art qualifications. For several years he was a stained glass designer. He then became art master at Armstrong College, Newcastle until 1906 when he came to Ipswich as Principal of the School of Art. He married Edith Ash of Gateshead-on-Tyne and had two daughters.

In 1897 he sent his first painting, from 10 Neville Street, Newcastle-upon-Tyne, to the Royal Academy entitled *The Widow*. He exhibited there again in 1911 and continously up to 1942.

During his vacations Rushton went on sketching tours in Britain and on the Continent. He visited Wales, Yorkshire, Wiltshire, Hampshire and Kent. He continued to work on commissions for large-scale "decorative work" at this time. After 1929 he retired to Blewbury, near Didcot Berkshire, where he produced many landscape watercolours of the area. His tours abroad took him mainly to the South of France and Belgium.

After a short period at Dedham, Essex, Rushton returned to Ipswich in 1936, where he remained at Upgrove, Belstead until his death. Rushton was a full member of the Royal Society of British Artists, of the Royal Birmingham Society of Artists and of the Royal Institute of Painters in Water Colour. He was an active member of the Ipswich Art Club from 1907 to 1948. His work is represented in the Birmingham City Art Galleries as well as in Ipswich.

This watercolour, which shows the play of light on the surfaces of the leaves and petals of the oleander stems, is a highly decorative composition. Rushton's knowledge of stained-glass design could have influenced his use of the translucent watercolour medium, of which he is clearly a technical master.

References:
EADT: 4.2.1929 Retirement from School of Art
Newspaper cutting of 1948: Obituary (Ipswich Museums)

GEORGE RUSHTON (1868-1948)

36 Tuddenham (Suffolk) 1925

Watercolour 40 x 57cm.
Signed, bottom right: *G. R. RUSHTON*
(R1925-135)

This was shown in the Ipswich Art Club exhibition of 1925 and was presented to Ipswich Museums by Sir Edward Packard.

At his retirement ceremony in 1929, Rushton paid tribute to "Many of the students [who] had come through the School very creditably, and had made good progress since". He especially mentioned **Leonard Squirrell,** whom he first knew as "a boy of fourteen". The correspondent for the East Anglian Daily Times described his continued speech as follows:

"He [Squirrell] had unusual qualities, both as a man and as an artist. In his special line of art, he considered Squirrell was one of the best technicians in the country — and of course he was much more than that, he was an artist".

Rushton was presented with a pastel by Squirrell of *Norwich Market Place* "a picture for which Mr. Rushton had expressed a preference".

Rushton was greatly appreciated by his students who remembered "the many little extra things" he had done for them, especially those "who had the pleasure and privilege of sketching with him on Summer afternoons". His obituary of 1948 in the local paper later described Rushton as a man "who had the gift of imparting his enthusiasm to others, of bringing out and directing latent talent, a man who by precept and practice fostered the application of art to everyday things". His watercolour technique in landscape painting, his greatest love, was absorbed by several students who made a name for themselves later. Amongst these were **Leonard Squirrell,** Reginald Haggar (1905-1988) Arthur Southgate (1905-1982), Albert Ribbans (1903-1966) George R. Fathers (1898-1968) and Elsie Haward (1882-1956).

Most of Rushton's landscape work shows wide vistas of rural scenery with powerful moving skies in all kinds of weather. When depicting architectural features, he well understood how light reflected from textural surfaces and how to convey the season or time of day through harmonious combinations of glowing colours. He looked at the broad aspect rather than the particular details of topography or items of human interest, which Leonard Squirrell developed in his work.

References:
See Plate 35.

BERTRAM PRIESTMAN (1868-1951)

37 **Walberswick Marshes** 1921

Oil on canvas 59 x 70.8cm.

Signed and dated, bottom left: *B. Priestman 21.*

(R1928-185)

This picture could be the one which appeared at the Royal Academy in 1927. It was shown at the Ipswich Art Club exhibition in 1928, where it was bought by Ipswich Museums.

Bertram Priestman was born in Bradford, the son of Edward and Henrietta Priestman, who were Quakers. His father was a director of the family woollen business and a local connoisseur and collector of paintings. He was educated at the Friends' School at Oliver's Mount, Scarborough and at Bootham, York, and enjoyed painting during the holidays with his uncle Arnold Pristman. From 1883 to 1886, while in York, he took lessons in watercolour painting with Edwin Moore and in oils with Mr Walton of Stonegate.

After he left school, Priestman went on a tour of Italy, Egypt and Palestine. On his return he began an engineering course at Bradford Technical College, but gave up to study at the Slade School in London for two terms under Alphonse Legros. In 1889 he worked in the studio of William Llewellyn (1858-1941), a member of the New English Art Club, who painted occasionally at Walberswick (see Plate 30).

Priestman exhibited at the Liverpool Academy in 1888, at the Royal Academy from 1890 and at the New English Art Club from 1894, of which he became a member in 1897. He also sent work to the Royal Society of British Artists.

In 1892 Priestman took a studio at Chiswick where he met Charles E. Holloway (1838-1897), whose broad handling of rich colour on his East Coast seascapes may have influenced his work. He had a life long admiration of James McNeill Whistler and was closely involved with Whistler's International Society. The work of William Maris, a Dutch painter of rural farmyard scenes, also fascinated him after a trip to Holland in 1895.

In 1914 Priestman moved to 'Windy Haugh' at Walberswick. After a period away in Wharfedale, he returned in 1919 and stayed until 1927 when he moved to Snape Hall and later Woodbridge. After 1923 he gave art lessons to Edward Seago (1910-1974) who thought Priestman was "a sound and sincere painter whose pictures were like the man — gentle, sincere and completely honest". The two often concentrated on skies and clouds on their sketching expeditions.

In 1851 the *Times* wrote:

"Priestman was primarily a naturalistic landscape painter, working in the English tradition that derives from Constable . . . . . . He had . . . . . . a subtle appreciation of atmosphere, a good control over colour, and above all, a fine command of cloud forms".

Bibliography:

Bertram Priestman (Exh. cat. Bradford Art Galleries & Museums & Ferens Art Gallery Hull, 1981)

Goodman, J., *Edward Seago: The Other Side of the Canvas* (Norwich, 1990)

References:

The Times: 20.3.1951 Obituary; Notes by the artist's daughter Miss D. Priestman 1973, (Ipswich Museums).

SIR ALFRED J. MUNNINGS (1878-1959)

38 **Travellers** 1910

Oil on canvas 76.5 x 126.8cm.

Signed, bottom left: *A. J. Munnings*
                                    1910

(R1911-10)

This was shown at the Ipswich Art Club exhibition of 1911, where it was purchased by Ipswich Museums.

Alfred Munnings was the second son of John Munnings, a miller of Mendham, Suffolk. After his education at Redenhall Grammar School and Framlingham College, his artistic talents led him into a six year apprenticeship with Page Brothers, a firm of lithographers in Norwich. After work every evening, he studied at the Norwich School of Art under Gertrude Offord, a watercolour painter of flowers. At Page's, Munnings was responsible for the advertisements for A. J. Caley & Sons, the chocolate manufacturers. John Shaw Tomkins, a director of Caley's, became Munnings' first patron. From 1897, Munnings began to exhibit with the Norwich Art Club and he was also a member of the Ipswich Art Club from 1899.

Tomkins took Munnings to Europe, visiting The Hague, Amsterdam and Berlin on the way to the Leipzig fair where Caley's had a stand. Following this trip, Munnings painted his first pictures to be accepted at the Royal Academy in 1898. After completing his apprenticeship, Munnings bought a carpenter's shop in Mendham and converted it into a studio. At about this time, he lost the sight of one eye, which was wounded by a briar while he helped a dog over a hedge. To increase his income, Munnings worked as a free-lance poster designer.

In 1902 and 1903 he went to study for short periods in Paris at the Academie Julian, but stayed at Mendham until 1904 when he moved to Church Farm Swainsthorpe and built a new studio. From here Munnings went on painting trips into the Ringland Hills in Norfolk, and to Hoxne, on the River Waveney in Suffolk. *Travellers,* illustrated here, would have been painted in these districts where he roamed with several horses and ponies, a caravan and a cart for his painting materials managed by his man Bob and a gypsy boy named Shrimp, all his models. They appear in other works by Munnings of this period e.g. *Augereau and Shrimp,* 1908 (Munnings Collection, Castle House, Dedham).

In 1910 he visited Newlyn in Cornwall and in 1911 he took a studio there. He also went to Hampshire to paint the gypsy hop-pickers.

Munnings became an official war artist in 1918, attached to the Canadian Cavalry Brigade. The success of this work ensured him of a great number of equestrian commissions after the war and changed his career.

In 1919 Munnings purchased Castle House, Dedham, where he lived for the rest of his life. In the following year he married Violet McBride a well-known horsewoman. In 1944 he was elected President of the Royal Academy and was knighted. A keen rider from youth, horses dominated Munning's canvases, in hunting, racing and fairground scenes.

Bibliography:
Booth, S., *Sir Alfred Munnings 1878-1959* (London, 1986)

ANNA AIRY (1882-1964)

39 **Interior with Mrs. Charles Burnand** 1919

Oil on canvas 76.2 x 63.5cm.
Signed and dated, bottom right: *A. Airy 1919*
(R1974-52)

This was presented to Ipswich Museums by Mrs. M. C. Burnand, the daughter-in-law of the sitter, in 1975. The Burnands were friends of Anna Airy in London.

Anna Airy was born in London, the daughter of Wilfred and Anna Airy (who died in childbirth). Wilfred was the son of Sir George Biddell Airy (1801-1892) the Astronomer Royal.

Anna remembered her father saying to her "that if I persisted in going in for art when I left school that he would give me the finest art education either in this country or on the Continent that could be had at the time after which I must stand on my own feet". In 1899 she entered the Slade School and during her five years there she was awarded not only the Slade Scholarship, but also the Melville Nettleship Prize for three consecutive years. She also won all the first prizes awarded at the School.

Her outstanding academic ability in art was recognised by many art institutions. From 1905 she regularly exhibited at the Royal Academy. In 1906 she was elected a Member of the Pastel Society, in 1908 an Associate of the Royal Society of Painter-Etchers and in 1909 a Member of the Royal Institute of Oil Painters. In 1913 she was made a Member of the Royal Society of Portrait Painters and in 1918 a Member of the Royal Institute of Painters in Water Colour. In 1916 she married Geoffrey Buckingham Pocock (1879-1960), a landscape artist.

During the First World War, Anna Airy was employed as a war artist. She produced possibly her most outstanding canvases, of munitions factories and women working in a Gas Retort House, for the British War Memorial Committee, the Imperial War Museum Committee and the Women's Work Committee. However, after the War she concentrated on figure compositions (sometimes twentieth century versions of the "Conversation Piece"), landscapes, flower pieces and still life. She was versatile in all media, working equally well in oils, watercolours, pastel, etching and crayon.

Interior with Mrs Charles Burnand is not just a portrait of a lady in her grand sitting room full of fine objects of interest. It is mainly intended as a study in composition and reflected light for which the figure and objects are only a vehicle. Anna Airy's dexterity with her brushes created highlights and the illusion of three dimensions, making this a showpiece of technical skill. Mrs Burnand, by the fireside, is painted without Anna's usual meticulous handling and recalls similar figures in interiors by Harold Gilman (1876-1919), a member of the Camden Town Group which evolved around 1911. It is possible that she was going through an experimental phase, as there are few other known works of this type by her. The images of mirrors and windows, which bounce back on to the large mirror facing the viewer, are calculated to create a sense of the space beyond the sitting room.

After 1933 Anna Airy and her husband moved to The Cottage, Playford near Ipswich. In 1945 she was elected President of the Ipswich Art Club, a position she held until her death.

Bibliography:

Webber, M., *Anna Airy R.I., R.O.I., R.E.* (Ipswich Art Club & Ipswich Museums, 1985)

LEONARD SQUIRRELL (1893-1979)

40 **A Corner of Old Paris** 1926

Pastel 51.4 x 73.5cm.

Signed and dated, bottom right: *L. R. Squirrell. 1926*

(R1926-101)

This was purchased from the Ipswich Art Club exhibition in 1926 by Ipswich Museums.

As a boy, Leonard Russell Squirrell lived at 82 Spring Road, Ipswich with his brother and widower father, a carpenter and joiner. In 1908 he joined the Ipswich School of Art as a full-time student, having been personally recommended by **George Rushton** the Principal, who visited Ipswich schools to select potential pupils. Years later Squirrell considered that he had been "well instructed in the principles of good design and composition and the art of picture making, apart from the entire range of general art school subjects" at the Art School. In 1913 he had a watercolour shown at the Royal Academy exhibition. Rushton employed Charles Baskett, A.R.E. (1845-1929), the retired head of Colchester School of Art, to run etching classes. Baskett taught Squirrell all the etching methods and they became great friends. In 1915, the year in which he won the British Institution Scholarship in Engraving, and 1922 they travelled together to Venice and in 1929, when Baskett died, Squirrell was his natural successor to teach etching at the School of Art (until 1940). In 1923 his prints, which sold through the dealer H. C. Dickins of London and the U.S.A., had made him enough money to get married. He and Hilda Bird set up home in Foxhall Road (and later at 46, Crabbe Street). In that year Squirrell received the Silver Medal of the International Printmaker's Exhibition in Los Angeles for his mezzotint *The High Mill*. He received gold medals there in 1925 and 1930 for *Notre Dame, Paris* another mezzotint, and *The Shadowed Corner Marseilles*, an aquatint.

While still a student at the Ipswich School of Art, he spent all of his own time sketching outdoors. He later wrote: "The granaries and maltings in Fore Street, with their piles of sacks and dusty rafters, provided many a subject and trained my hand to draw. I emphasise that because, as mainly a topographical artist, good drawing has been the aim and the substance of my whole career".

After the War, in 1918, he returned to the Ipswich School of Art for a couple of years and went on to the Slade in London. There he studied under Henry Tonks (1862-1937), **Philip Wilson Steer** and Sir Walter Russell (1867-1949).

After leaving the Slade, Squirrell visited the Continent. This was mainly at the expense of Mr. Kerner-Greenwood, a factory owner at Kings Lynn who until his death in 1927, employed Squirrell to produce advertisement graphics for his "Pudlo" cement water-proofer. W. F. Greeves, an avid collector of Squirrell's pictures from 1928, later described the European work, which included a sketchbook of Venice and "quiet corners of Marseilles, Avignon, and the pictures of Provence, the Maritime Alps, Sospel, Eze and Ventmiglia. He likes to depict street scenes where the rigid line of architecture and the pleasing, because skilful, introduction of figures afford scope for his drawing. Such scenes he recorded in Paris, Rouen and Dieppe".

Bibliography:
Walpole, J., *Leonard Squirrell: A Biographical Scrapbook* (Suffolk, 1982)
Butler, P., *Leonard Squirrell R.W.S., R.E.* (Exh. cat. Ipswich Art Club & Ipswich Museum, 1978)

LEONARD SQUIRRELL (1893-1979)

41 Kersey, Suffolk 1928

Pastel 40.4 x 40.4cm.

Signed and dated, bottom right: *L. R. Squirrell. 1928.*

(R1928-186)

This was purchased from the Ipswich Art Club exhibition in 1928 by Ipswich Museums.

Squirrell became a master of the faceted surface, drawing chalk pits, quarries, ravines, demolition sites and urban panoramas illuminated by a coloured mosaic of sunshine and shadow. He would have learned a great deal about the play of light and shade from **George Rushton,** who became a sketching companion as well as his teacher. Rushton, a stained-glass designer and watercolourist, well understood the subtleties of reflected and transparent light falling on and passing through the varying planes in his subjects (see 35). The teaching of Steer and Russell, inspired by the French Impressionist ideas of transient light and atmosphere would have played their part. Squirrell shared an admiration for the watercolours of John Sell Cotman with his best friend the artist Frederick Baldwin (1899-1984) whom he met in 1923. They often visited the Colman collection of Cotmans in Norwich together, absorbing Cotman's technique of creating simplified flattened forms with areas of plain delicate colour, imperceptibly separated by the white of the paper.

Although watercolour and etching appear to have been Squirrell's favourite media, he also produced a lot of pastels, especially during the 1920's. He rarely worked in oil and hardly ever painted watercolours or pastels on the spot. He prepared pencil sketches outdoors instead, marking them with colour keys and notes which later would be interpreted in his studio where the final picture was prepared. Baldwin had some memories of Squirrell's pastel work.

"I think he gave up pastels as there seemed no satisfactory way of fixing ..... This was caused because he liked to use pastel as drawing and not rubbed to give a smooth finish. But he did some fine things in the medium. I remember one in particular which was produced in the *Studio* called 'The Tall Red House Dieppe'. Anyway, I think he gave up his membership of the Pastel Society and reverted to his favourite medium [i.e. watercolour]".

James Mason Martin of Ipswich was another important patron of Squirrell. The Martin family still owns two pastels produced in the 1920's, *The Gateway Framlingham Castle* (1924) and *Autumn Sunshine, Bramford* (1927).

Squirrell's publications included *Landscape Painting in Pastel* (1939) and *Practice in Watercolour* (1950). During his lifetime he exhibited regularly at the Royal Academy and the Royal Society of Painters in Watercolours. (He was a member of the Royal Institute of Painters in Watercolours between 1933 and 1935). He was for many years a Fellow of the Royal Society of Painter — Etchers and Engravers. He produced posters for the regional railway companies (before they became British Railways), the Brewer's Society, and the British Travel and Holidays Association. He also drew for the Oxford University Press's annual *Almanack*.

Although he toured through Scotland, the north of England and the Continent, it is for his distinctive portrayals of the villages and churches of East Anglia that he is best remembered.

Bibliography:
See Plate 40

KERSEY Suffolk

L R Squirrell
1928

JOHN MILLAR WATT (1895-1975)

42 **Higham from Langham** c1927

Oil on canvas 57.3 x 64.8cm.

Signed, bottom right: *MILLAR WATT*

(R1927-71)

This was purchased from the Ipswich Art Club exhibition of 1927 by Ipswich Museums.

John Millar Watt was born in Gourock on the Clyde but was educated in Ilford and later at the Cass Art Institute, London. He joined the advertising agency of Mather & Crowther and succeeded Tom Purvis the poster designer. During the First World War, Millar Watt joined the Artists' Rifles in 1915 and in 1916 was commissioned in the Essex Regiment. After 1918 he studied art at the Slade School and began to contribute sports cartoons to the *Daily Chronicle*.

He was employed as an artist on the *Daily Sketch* and created the prototype of his cartoon character "POP" in 1921, "The rotund, bald, bespatted figure sporting top hat, cravat and tail coat".

The character appeared in the *Daily Sketch* for over twenty-five years and was popular with King George V and Winston Churchill.

Millar Watt was also a landscape painter and, while living at Dedham, went out sketching and painting with **Sir Alfred Munnings** who once wrote: "I have the greatest admiration for Millar Watt both as an artist and as a man". Millar Watt exhibited at the Royal Academy in 1936 and 1937 and his wife, Amy Maulby Biggs (1929-1953), a landscape and flower painter, also exhibited work there and at the Paris Salon. They were both members of the Ipswich Art Club from the mid-1920's to 1935.

Millar Watt lived in "active retirement" in Lavenham, Suffolk. He was also an expert on painting materials and methods of painting by the Old Masters. Apparently "an imposing copy of *Bacchus and Ariadne* by Millar Watt was a prominent feature in his hall at Lavenham".

References:
The Times: 17.2.1975 Obituary
Ipswich Evening Star: 19.12.1975
Images Magazine (Ipswich): Nov/Dec 1989 A Family of Artists (Ipswich)

GEORGE R. FATHERS (1898-1968)

43 **Sun Up** 1921

Pencil and watercolour 21.8 x 26.6cm.

Signed and dated, bottom right: *G. FATHERS 21.*

(R1921-85)

This was purchased from the Ipswich Art Club exhibition of 1921 by Mr. T. Partington Jnr who presented it to Ipswich Museums that year.

George Fathers was born in Derby, the son of Caleb Fathers a master plasterer and sculptor. He was educated in Ipswich and later at Hitchin. Fathers attended the Ipswich School of Art under **George Rushton** between 1918 and 1922. He would have met **Leonard Squirrell** (who was completing his studies at the Art School for a couple of years after the War), and Charles Baskett (1845-1929) would have taught him the etching process there. Rushton's early influence on Fathers as a watercolourist is evident in *Sun Up,* which was painted while he was a student in Ipswich, and shows a similar understanding of soft atmospheric light on the landscape (see Plate 36). Fathers went on to the Royal College of Art from 1922 to 1925 where he studied under Professor William Rothenstein (1872-1945). In June 1924 he contributed an illustration to the RCA Students Magazine called *The Bathers.* In 1925 he sent his first and only picture to the Royal Academy, called *628 Regent Street 1925.* At this time he was living at 59 Redcliffe Road, London SW10. He also exhibited with the New English Art Club.

According to *Who's Who in Art* he became an art manager in a publishing house and a director and art director in process engraving from 1930 to 1940, although the name of the company for which he worked is not known. He was also a visiting teacher at the Borough Polytechnic Hull and Leeds College of Art. From at least 1945 to 1946 he was living in Leeds but from 1948 until his death he lived at 33 Haworth Road, Heaton, Bradford. He was a trustee of the Bradford Art Club for many years, and exhibited annually in the Spring Exhibition of Modern British Paintings and Sculpture at Cartwright Hall in Bradford from 1945 to 1958. He produced oils and pastels as well as watercolours of mainly landscape views, often of the Yorkshire dales or coast. Titles of his exhibits in Bradford indicate that he spent holidays in Rotterdam, the Channel Islands and Spain. He was a member of the Ipswich Art Club from 1921 to 1963.

References:
Catalogues of the Spring Exhibition of Modern British Paintings and Sculpture, Cartwright Hall, Bradford (Bradford Local Studies Library).
Records of Cremations at Nabwood Cemetery near Bradford.
Who's Who in Art eds. 1960 to 1970.
RCA Student's Magazine, vol ii, no viii, June 1924. (Royal College of Art Archive).

Bibliography

(See also under Suffolk artist's sections)

Allthorpe-Guyton, M., with Stephens, J., *A Happy Eye: A School of Art in Norwich 1845-1982* (Norwich, 1982)

Beckett, R. B., ed., *John Constable's Correspondence* Vols I, II & VI (Ipswich, 1962-8)

Bennett, C., *Christchurch Mansion & Park Ipswich: An Illustrated Souvenir* (Ipswich, 1989)

Blatchly, J., *The Topographers of Suffolk,* 5th edition, (Suffolk Record Office, 1988)

Collins, I., *A Broad Canvas: Art in East Anglia since 1880* (Norwich, 1990)

Day, H., *East Anglian Painters* Vol I (Eastbourne, 1967)

Dictionary of National Biography (entries for Josiah Whymper and Edwin Edwards)

Fox, C., & Greenacre, F., *Artists of the Newlyn School 1880-1900* (Exh, cat. Newlyn & Bristol Art Galleries, 1979)

Hayes, J., *Gainsborough* (London, 1975)

Hermann, L., & Owen, F., *Sir George Beaumont of Coleorton, Leicestershire* (Leicester Museum & Art Gallery, c1970)

Houfe, S., *Charles Keene of Punch* (Exh, cat. Christies London, 1991)

Ipswich Art Club, *Loan Exhibition & Works by Gainsborough, Constable and*

Old Suffolk Artists at the Art Gallery, Ipswich (Exh. cat., 1887) (Suffolk Record Office)

Jobson., *Walberswick Story* (Lowestoft, 1953)

Layard, G. S., *The Life & Letters of Charles Keene* (London, 1892)

Leslie, C. R., *Memoirs of the Life of John Constable* (London, 1951)

Moore, A. W., *The Norwich School of Artists* (Norfolk Museums, 1985)

Morfey, W. M., *A Brief View of the History of Ipswich School* (Ipswich School, 1984)

Orpen, W., ed., *The Outline of Art* (London, 1957)

Parkin, M., *Mark Senior 1864-1927 of Leeds & Runswick Bay* (Exh. cat. Michael Parkin Gallery London, 1974)

Parry, A., & Webber, M., *Centenary Exhibition of the Ipswich Art Club 1874-1974* (Ipswich, 1975)

Robins, A., *The New English Art Club Centenary Exhibition* (Exh. cat. Christies London, 1986)

Walker, H., *The Ipswich Institute 1824-1924* (Ipswich, 1924)

Woolner, A., *Thomas Woolner R.A. Sculptor & Poet, His Life in Letters* (London, 1917)

References

(From the Suffolk Record Office) N.B. Ipswich Journal = IJ, Suffolk Chronicle = SC, East Anglian Daily Times = EADT

Jabez Hare Jnr: IJ: 4.3.1837 Notice of death; SC: 29.4.1837 Advertisement for a memorial tablet; Fitch Suffolk Collection Vols 3 & 4 17.3.1837 Obituary notice.

Robert Clamp: IJ: 3.7.1819 Academy advertisement; IJ: 11.1.1823 Academy advertisement; IJ: 27.5.1826 E. Smythe's prize for drawing.

Edward FitzGerald/Perry Nursey: East Anglian Miscellany Vols 40-44 No 11,502 (1946) p.32 Link with other artists

John Smart: IJ: 29.9.1858 Mechanics' Institute reports death

W. T. Griffiths: EADT: 14.5.1906 Retirement

Mechanics Institute: Minute Book containing transcriptions of lectures (HD116:2861)

Ipswich Society of Professional & Amateur Artists: Minute Book 1832-1837 (K13/1/10)

Ipswich School of Art: SC: 29.1.1859 Advertisement; IJ: 1.2.1859 Editorial Comment; SC: 2.3.1861 Article about work of students.

Suffolk Association of Fine Arts: IJ: 31.8.1850; 21.9.1850; 20.9.1851; 18.9.1852; EADT: 22.1.1890; T. B. Ross's *Chronicles of Ipswich 1848-1850* (qSIps352).

Acknowledgements

The production of this book would not have been possible without the support and help of many people. The following are thanked for their important contributions: Joe Orr, Director of Leisure Services, Ipswich Borough Council and Sara Muldoon, Curator of Ipswich Borough Museums & Galleries, for authorising the expenditure on this venture and for allowing me to write the book as part of the Museum's work programme; Mel Birch of *Images Publications* who, as co-publisher and the designer, has organised the printing work with a wealth of enthusiasm, commitment and creative ideas; Blair Potter, Museum Custodian, for his perceptive guidance on financial aspects and picture selection; Douglas Atfield for the excellent photography; Barbara Husk, Dr. John Blatchly, Wallace Morfey, Richard Scott and Adrian Parry, Secretary of the Ipswich Art Club, who have kindly and generously shared their own research and records without hesitation; Chris Reeve, Fine Arts Research Assistant St. Edmundsbury Borough Museums; Lord Tollemache; Christine Hopper, Assistant Keeper of Art, Bradford Art Galleries & Museums; Elvira Willmott, Specialist Librarian — Local Studies, Bradford Libraries & Information Service; Andrea Ellis, Secretary of the Bradford Arts Club; the staffs of Essex and Suffolk County Libraries, the Suffolk Record Office, Derbyshire Record Office and Derby Local Studies Library; Eugene Rae, Royal College of Art Archive; John Fairclough, Educational Liaison Officer, Museum Education Service, Suffolk County Council, for proof reading my typescript and Juliette Farthing at the Ipswich Museum on the word-processor. Any errors in this volume are entirely my own responsibility.